Growth to selfhood

Also by A. Reza Arasteh

Rumi the Persian, the Sufi

Growth to Selfhood

The Sufi contribution

A. Reza Arasteh

Routledge & Kegan Paul
London, Boston and Henley

First published in 1980
by Routledge & Kegan Paul Ltd
39 Store Street, London WC1E 7DD,
Broadway House, Newtown Road,
Henley-on-Thames, Oxon RG9 1EN and
9 Park Street, Boston, Mass. 02108, USA
Set in 11-13 pt Baskerville by
Ronset Ltd, Darwen, Lancs
and printed in Great Britain by
Redwood Burn Ltd
Trowbridge & Esher

British Library Cataloguing in Publication Data

Arasteh, A. Reza,

Growth to selfhood.
1. Sufism
I. Title
181'.5   BP189.2   79-41238

ISBN 0 7100 0355 2

Contents

Contents

Acknowledgments

The author and the publishers are grateful for permission to reprint passages from the following copyright material:
Jalalu'ddin Rumi, *The Mathnawi* (translated by R. A. Nicholson), 1926, 1930, by permission of Cambridge University Press, New York;
Iqbal, *The Reconstruction of Religious Thought in Islam*, 1962, and Al-Ghazzali, *The Confession* (n.d.), by permission of Ashraf Press, Lahore;
Attar, *Muslim Saints and Mystics* (trans. A. J. Arberry), Routledge & Kegan Paul Ltd, 1966.

Introduction

This study deals with the patterns and processes of growth to selfhood in the Sufis, a group of Near Eastern mystics who analysed the underlying realities of religion, philosophy and science and unveiled the mysteries of man's psyche as a means of attaining perfection and certainty. Sufism developed the art of transcending one's self to perfection, thereby contributing greatly to an understanding of personality development and the discovery of self.

In essence, Sufism develops in the individual a process of continual rebirth until he attains real selfhood. The question then arises: what is this self which the Sufis would like to realize?

According to Sufism the real self is not what environment and culture develop in us, but it is basically the product of the universe in evolution. I shall refer to it henceforth as cosmic self or universal self in contrast to phenomenal self, the product of culture and environment. Cosmic self can be thought of as the image of the universe which must be unveiled. It is wrapped in our unconscious, if it is not the unconscious itself, whereas the phenomenal self encompasses consciousness. In Sufism the cosmic unconscious receives more importance than consciousness; it possesses infinite potentialities, while consciousness is limited; and only the unconscious provides the means of attaining the real self. The cosmic self embraces all our being while the phenomenal self designates only a part of our existence. The phenomenal self has separated us from our origin, that of union with all of life. Having now become aware of

this separation, we can only live fully by emptying consciousness, bringing to light the unconscious, achieving insight into
our whole existence and living in a state of complete awareness.
I shall call this state cosmic existence or transcendental
consciousness. The real self can be thought of as the crown of
unconsciousness, which is potentially conscious existence, the
Sufi's goal.[1] To identify this psychic state is not ordinarily
easy, for its very nature is one of becoming, and when attained
that is fulfilment. Persian Sufis believe that it is self-explanatory
and self-evident. Just as the sun is proof of itself, so too is the
real self. Each of us has at some time experienced it. At least
once we have heard its voice, its call, and its invitation,[2] often
without our realization. Perhaps the words 'me', 'he' or 'it' can
better identify the real self than 'I' or 'we'. In this sense
Sufism consists of two steps: (1) the passing away of 'I', and
(2) becoming wholly aware of 'me'. The real self exists in no
place, its very nature is intensive rather than extensive, and
it can be both near us and far removed, depending on the
individual's experience. Ordinarily a flash of knowledge
enlightens the consciousness, a small circle of our psyche, but
when we attain the real self a strong flash constantly illuminates the whole structure of our psyche. Some Sufis give the
heart[3] as its site, but one may ask, 'How can the heart, meaning
really an ability for intuitive experience, have a definite
locus?' In the following poem Rumi designates its source if not
its location:[4]

Cross and Christians, from end to end,
I surveyed; He was not on the cross.
I went to the idol-temple, to the ancient pagoda;
No trace was visible there.

---

[1] At this point the Sufi is called *Safi*, the pure one.
[2] Ordinary speech tends to obscure the meaning of Sufism. In their
writings Sufis have resorted to an allegorical style to express their thoughts.
I have followed this practice frequently in this study.
[3] The heart as the source of understanding acquires awareness by insight
or a sudden psychical leap.
[4] Jalalalddin Rumi, *Divan-i Shams Tabriz, Selected Poems*, ed. and trans.
R. A. Nicholson, Cambridge, 1898, p. 10.

I went to the mountains of Herat and Candahor[5] [Ghandehar]*;*
I looked, He was not in that hill or dale.
With set purpose I fared to the summit of Mount Qaf[6]
In that place was only Anga's habitation.
I bent the reins of search to the Ka'aba[7]
He was not in that resort of Old and Young.
I questioned Ibn Sina of His state;
He was not within Ibn Sina's range,[8]
I fared towards the scene of two bow-lengths' distance,
He was not in that exalted court.
I gazed into my heart;
There I saw Him; He was nowhere else.

The above poem describes the Sufis' search for the site of the
real self. Not finding it in various religions, reason or other
sources, he at last discovers it within himself.

Can one achieve the state of cosmic self by being taught its
principles? No, not at all in the sense that conventional
knowledge cannot transform the inner self. Thus experience
offers the only way. The Sufis undoubtedly rely heavily on
inner experience and accepted religious practices.

The one who seeks to transform his social self must experience
at least once what he is seeking. He must become aware of
the problems of human existence: what are we? What is our
destination and why? He must sense his origin and become
aware of the fact that with all our strivings we don't know why
we, like fish, have been cast into a net allowing us endless
views of the world. At this point the individual senses that he
once lived in closer harmony with nature.

In such a state we must become genuinely interested in ourselves and know the nature of our true self. We must therefore
become conscious of the make-up of our conventional self,
know its structure and try to become aware of its positive and

---

[5] In Afghanistan.
[6] Qaf, the residence of Simurgh, who is identical to God and is the object of
search of unification in 'Attar's *Mantiq ul Tair*, a mystical text.
[7] 'The Ka'aba' exemplifies religion.
[8] 'Ibn Sina's range' exemplifies the range of intellect.

negative qualities. To change our conventional self and transcend its state requires a conscientious effort. In this effort a sincere religious belief and its practice can become a transitional mechanism for self-growth. Thus, conventional religion becomes a beginning. Depending on the state of the psyche of the seeker, conventional religious belief can lead to identification with the Creator or at least with His attributes. This effort brings us to the threshold of selfhood, to the moment of resolution, and commitment. It is at this stage that knowledge and conceptualization, and Aristotelian logic are found to be helpless. What shall we do then? The Sufis have developed a dual mechanism of behavioural and psychical experience under the guidance of a true guide in order to reach selfhood and affirm it by a greater experience of *An,* the climax of our being.

This study is an attempt to assist 'man' to grow to his or her selfhood, and it is dedicated to my late Master Ellahi Qumushai of Tehran as well as to my grandfather Baba Mirza, who inspired me. May peace be with them.

Chapter I
The organic nature of self in Sufism

Unlike Western psychologists and psychoanalysts who have limited themselves in depth and dimension to the familial, social, and occasionally to the historical self, the Sufis give an infinite and unlimited potential to self, which extends from the unknown point of creation (*azal*) to the unknown point of eternity (*abad*) – way beyond the death-bed. One's root of self is not in America, Persia or Africa. It is beyond the inorganic earth and beyond the time of the earth's formation. Which galaxy our origin is in and where that galaxy came from are still mysteries. To which galaxy we eventually will turn and what will happen then are still mysteries. However, by charting the self's dimensions and its course, believing in its continuity and relating its earthly life to its heavenly course, the Sufis definitely provided a better inner comfort and certainty for man than objective science and the argumentation of philosophers.

The Sufis believed, though intuitively, that it has taken man a million years to evolve to his present condition. First, we were in a state of inorganic things, and from that state of the inorganic we evolved to a vegetative state. Many centuries we lived in this state of vegetation until we forgot that we once were solid. Then from a vegetative state, we evolved into an animal state, and we forgot about our previous state, even though every spring we have an inclination toward sweet herbs and clover. Finally, from the animal state we evolved towards humanity. Though creative action was there before Adam was born, we hardly remember. Now from conception we pass through birth, but we fail to remember the recreation of the universe which took place in the mother's womb. From birth we pass through socialization, develop a social self, and forget our purpose. If lucky, we specialize and repeat ourselves and forget our creative potential. We develop an ego which will block our growth. If by chance we objectify our ego and the role of family, society and culture, we may find a way to know the origin of culture in terms of creativity. Thus we will, if persistent, relate our own creative acts to cosmic creativity by producing new forms externally and unfolding our 'selves' internally, finally attaining a state that original Sufis called conscious existence.

In other words, we must be born again and again, experience novelty again and again until we arrive at the state of selfhood. However, the faith in this growing potential requires that at one state of our growth we become aware of our conventional self, a process which requires years of preparation, experience, and interaction with generations of our parents and grandparents and generations of our children and grandchildren, and with the changing environment. Our ego and rationality mature through this process of social interaction. In turn, we must assimilate culture so completely that we become its representatives, for we can only objectify culture and wean ourselves from it after we have first absorbed it.

We realize the dimension of our self when we become aware of the fact that our historical self and conventional self constitute only a short span of evolution of our 'selves'. We then perceive the distance between our conventional self and our real self. Perception of this distance between our imitative parental self and our real self may awaken us and put us on the right path of growth to selfhood. This long path of growth is beautifully expressed in the following poem by the Master Sufi Jalalalddin Rumi, which I have entitled 'From No-Man to Cosmic Man':[1]

> *Low in the earth*
> *I lived in realms of ore and stone;*
> *And then I smiled in many-tinted flowers;*
> *Then roving with the wild and wandering hours,*
> *O'er earth and air and ocean's zone*
> > *In a new birth*
> > *I dived and flew,*
> > *And crept and ran.*
> *And all the secret of my essence drew*
> *Within a force that brought them all to view*
> *And lo, a man!*
> > *And then my goal.*
> *Beyond the clouds, beyond the sky,*
> *In realms where none may change or die –*
> *In angel form; and then away*
> *Beyond the bounds of night and day,*
> *And Life and Death, unseen or seen,*
> *Where all that is hath ever been,*
> > *As One and Whole.*

While Jalalalddin Rumi wrote a few poems about the evolutionary dimension of self, his predecessor Farid al Din, known as 'Attar (the Druggist), wrote a book about it.

'Attar, in his delightful book *Musibat Nama*, that is *Creative Suffering*, or in my understanding of its meaning, *Psychic Pain for Growth to Selfhood*, beautifully charts the course of inner evolution from the time of our separation from the cosmos and leads us to reunion with the cosmic sphere by a series of separation, anxiety, search and reunion. The central character in the book of *Creative Suffering* is of course a natural man, but not a doped, stoned, and slumbering man; an awakened man full of energy of anxiety of separation, who unconsciously is longing for the previous simple state of union after all. The character is an anxious searcher of the path of growth – inner growth. He represents the real situation of mankind, that is a psycho-religious being in search of his origin and in pursuit of his ultimate destiny. His situation is real and natural. Down in

3

the depths of his psyche he knows that once he was without existential pain and unconsciously related to all, but now that harmony is gone; he feels a distance between himself and the rest of nature. He feels pain, and knows that the present situation is not real, not comfortable, and he must seek a new harmony, a new union. In the first stage the seeker turns to the environment from which he had been separated. He seeks union by worshipping and relating to natural phenomena such as the sea, the sun, moon, wind, mountains, even soil and majestic trees. Each of these phenomena describe their own inadequacy and tell the seeker that they are unable to help him know himself. Somehow the seeker, after going through this process of primitive realism, experiences a relief from his pain and becomes aware of it, but finds himself in a wider horizon but with a greater pain from this new separation.

At this second stage the seeker turns toward the prophets. He seeks an answer to his natural self from Adam, Abraham, Moses, Christ and Muhammad. Adam speaks of his own sin and search, but refers the seeker to Abraham. Abraham advises him that salvation lies in hard work, but refers him to Moses. Moses tells him that patience is the key to the joy of selfhood, but refers him to Christ. Christ tells him that the path of purity leads him to the illumination of selfhood, but refers our seeker-representative to Muhammad. The Prophet advises him to seek selfhood within himself. He advises him that self-hood, like God, is closer than his jugular vein and he had better examine his powerful faculties: the senses, imagination, reason, heart and soul. When our representative questions the senses, they answer that as always they are erroneous and inadequate. The senses can only perceive the world of many, not unity, but refer the seeker to man's power of imagination. Imagination receives the question of man whole-heartedly but explains, 'though I enter the world of unity, I often find a unity based on an illusion'. Explaining the limitations of his power, imagination then refers our seeker to reason. Reason receives the question, reflects on it and tells our representative that undoubtedly he can give him some answer to man's urge to selfhood, but if he considers reason's response to be the entire answer then he is unreasonable. Then reason refers our seeker to his heart, the source of all man's quest. Heart receives our representative with great generosity and tells him that ideas which are not rooted in his domain of feelings can hardly materialize. Then heart tells our representative that he can only motivate his quest to reach the beloved soul. This realization initiates the path to selfhood.

Another way of looking at the dimension of self is by contrasting personal opinion, the power of appetite, to rationality and then seeking so much intellectualization, specialization and classification until every argument becomes meaningless. Finally, if we are awakened, we realize that no one can get drunk by knowing the word 'wine', and that no person can pluck a rose from 'rose'. In such a situation as the present-day state of our intellectuals and academicians, the awakened ones may seek wisdom through original experience. They may discover that their rationality and argumentation have produced a new sophisticism and irrationality which blocks their growth to selfhood. If perchance they see the light beyond limited intellectual experience and like Jalalalddin Rumi discover that the legs of logicians, philosophers and mechanical scientists are wooden, and wooden legs are untrustworthy – especially on the long path of growth to selfhood – then they may 'seek truth and shame the devil'.

Furthermore, an analysis of the dimension of self tells us that rational self by its nature is the product of man in history and is finite; self-wisdom is the product of an inner evolution and is congenial to the true nature of man and by its organic characteristics is infinite. Rational self is the product of the mental frame and its development. Real self is resultant from intuitive power and enlightened reason by its makeup is organic and illuminating. Rational self, when it achieves its peak, declines; it becomes an instrument in the hands of our impulses or it directs itself toward justice externally and further growth internally, depending on our habits and inclinations. On the other hand, the real self is rooted in our collective humanity, and its expression is nothing but in harmony with humankind's interests.

What we have presented so far is only a brief description of man's potential self, its dimension, its reality and its course of growth. We also have shown that what Sufi masters call self is beyond the scope of ordinary social and even rational self. But we have hardly touched the fact that the perception of real self, even insight into its existence, marks the initial conflict with our conventional self. So complicated is the nature of this conflict and so closely is its thread interwoven with the individual differences in our characters that it requires great courage to face it, and even more to deal with it. To become mature, we must strive to develop sufficient strength to stand up against undesirable mental blocks, to acquire the psychic fortitude (through prayer-meditation and practice of virtues) to resist undesirable environmental forces, and to set a new standard free of all that is held dear.

In psychoanalytic terms both C. G. Jung and Erich Fromm have explained how conventional self and conformity may bar man from fully developing his self to selfhood. Experimental youth of the 1960s noticed this matter but failed to realize the dimension of real self, because in a synthetic society they tried synthetic means without realizing that at the end they are drained of capacity, standing without any self. Sufis had a better way for transformation from conventional self to real self. Unlike psychoanalytic technique, they utilized religious behaviour, tasks for purification and removal of false values and false interest. We will discuss this intermediate technique in the next chapter. It will suffice here to say that the perception of the reality of real self in contrast to conventional self may make us realize that what we ordinarily call real is just a fiction, what we call truth is false. What we call personality is really that which shadows our potential personality and is in fact that which deprives our inner growth. That which we call self is really that which veils our 'self', and what to us is 'we' is only a barrier to becoming 'We'. In short, from conventional 'I' to real 'I', from conventional 'we' to real 'We' is a long way to go which requires freeing ourselves of undesirable desires and undesirable attitudes. The Sufis utilize the true function of religion for this transitional period; a subject for the next chapter.

Chapter 2
The structure and anatomy of conventional self

To Marx, religion was opium; to Freud, it was an illusion; but to the Sufis, religion was a useful step toward man's growth to selfhood. However, before discussing religion as a transitional mechanism for growth, we must analyse the structure of conventional self, because conventional self is a thesis, true religious practices an antithesis, and the Sufi self system a synthesis.

Structure of conventional self

The Sufis, as we briefly indicated in the introductory chapter, knew the conventional self as the product of social, historical, national and certainly personal impulses. The expression *nafs amará* (impulsive forces) was used for it. Conventional self can become the greatest barrier to the growth of man. It can cause regression in man, and can create a negative tendency in him. It can divert man's total energy toward unnecessary activities and make him believe deception as truth, fiction as reality and self-glorification as man's goal in life. One of the best examples of such a case was the former president of the United States, Richard Nixon. In our analysis, he was the smallest, the meanest and the lowest man who occupied the highest office in the transitional world. He was so blinded by personal impulses that, while he could immortalize himself in the history of his nation, he hadn't the power or insight to see this and had to sacrifice it for the immediate satisfaction of his conventional self.

The makeup of the conventional impulsive self is therefore very powerful, although its destructive effect differs from one individual to another.

Structurally, conventional self is a variety of selves. It includes:

1 parental selves
2 generational self
3 social self
4 professional self
5 fatherhood or motherhood
6 national self
7 historical self

The process of growth of the conventional self is itself often neglected, but we can try to chart its course for an average person. Normally, in order to succeed in any society and become a recognized member of that society, one must discover one's parental self and accept it. In this respect we again differ from Freud, who advocated that unless a man castrates his own father, he will not become an adult. We consider this view the unconscious impact of Freud's parents on his character structure, and the product of his Jewish tradition plus familial and cultural patterns. Discovery of the parental self is a step toward inner freedom, and acceptance of parents brings a greater freedom. This inner discovery and attachment is necessary, because without it we would always be in conflict with the parental superego. Furthermore, no normal person can change his or her parents. Each of us has only one father and one mother, but many friends, teachers or enemies. The sooner we realize this issue phenomenologically, the better for us. After all, parents are the instruments and begininng of our growth, not the end of it.

Likewise, we must participate in our generational self and become aware of it; from the age of three on, we grow in association with others. Each of our childhood friends brings to us his or her parental conventional self. We interchange images, interests, values, feelings, behaviours, conducts and many invisible qualities. In our youth, depending upon the characteristics of our environment, we generally revolt against our parental self, partly due to our generational self. Often the power of our generational self is so strong that we take issues up with our social, national and historical selves. The United States experienced this challenge in the 1960s, and the third world has been experiencing it since the end of the Second World War, if not before. However, selling our growth to our generational self is as unwise as blindly obeying our parental self. One's generational self must be discovered, just as one must discover one's familial self. Its value system must be identified, scrutinized and, if desirable, acted out. If helpful for further growth, it must be believed in; if not, it must be rejected, or at least one must become aware of it. One definitely must experience it, and then along with the familial self one must utilize it for the discovery of the social self.

The social self often is provincial, sectarian and limited to the ethnic group. This tribalism is one of the problems of the present-day world. On the other hand, the only way that one can transcend one's tribal social self is by identifying with it and discovering its relation to the national self. Unfortunately, due to social injustices and a great deal of prejudice, this detachment from the tribal self is not easy. Furthermore, the erroneous sectarian religions, whether Judaism, Christianity or Islam, have made tribal and social self a solid barrier to growth. In a homogeneous society, relating social self to national self is easy, but in a diversified society such growth is very difficult. Though people in the United States, as well as in Russia and Europe, are related to one another by constitution, laws and central government, their unconscious belonging which influences their social character is deeply rooted in their so-called 'own people'.

I have often felt that America as a nation was formed to produce universal men like Jefferson; but alas, it has a long way to go to utilize Jefferson's image as a national self. A new tribalism is in the making. Hopefully, each one of us will discover his tribal self, transcend it and at least discover Jefferson's self as a man. I once entertained a well-educated

Jewish friend who sincerely believed that he was first a Jew and second an American, though his ancestors had been so-called Americans.

Realization of the national self guides a social leader, if alert, to relate it to the historical self (our second mother). Then such a man may discover the futility of the historical self, and may stand at the threshold of history and laugh at history and history-makers.

It is this laughter which becomes the beginning of the Sufi's path to selfhood. However, the ingredients of the conventional self are often made of negative forces which hardly help us in the process of growth. On the contrary, we often grow up with mental blocks due to undesirable child-rearing, unwanted conception, unsuitable association, fragmentary knowledge and conflicting human relations. In such a case, a great number of barriers appear in our path.

These barriers can be classified in terms of (1) economic needs for food, shelter and clothing, and (2) our human relations. Definitely we are in need of food, though the master Sufi Rumi claimed: 'I eat the light which is the essence of the soul; I don't eat leg of lamb which is full of bones.' But many people live to eat instead of eating to live. Often emotional deprivation manifests itself in eating until one is enslaved by it. The sign of loss of will and mastery of appetite over people's desire is well-expressed in the habit of smoking. A healthy person forms only one habit; that is, forming no habit. It is enough to remind ourselves that a minority is enslaved by eating, and a majority is suffering from hunger. In general, we can safely conclude that the more appetite controls our affairs, the more polluted is the body. On the other hand, the purer the body, the more accurate the judgment of the organs for the demand of proper nutrition. The battle of correct nutrition and its impact on health has just started and undoubtedly will continue as people become interested in themselves. Experience dictates to us that the more peaceful we are, the less protein we require. On the other hand, the more neurotic we are, the more we become meat-eaters.

Regarding shelter, we still have not learned that one of the best ways of filling the vacuum between man and nature is by means of permanent architecture. Lack of insight into permanency makes man build under pressure and for profit. The result is that generation after generation becomes the slave of shelter. Like children, we build temporary shelters and are ready to wreck them any day. With regard to clothing, our judgment is no better than with shelter. However, even greater difficulty appears as a result of our human relations.

Erroneously, we believe that conflict is natural. We don't even stop to reflect on it. Suppose, for instance, that conflict is innate in us. Are we then here to increase its intensity by undesirable competition and harmful rivalry? Or are we here to try to keep it at the lowest level? I feel we are here to transform conflict into harmony. However, our lack of respect for one another, our misjudgment about sex and love, our insecurity in life and our projection of our impulses into fame and power all contribute to a large number of social ills. In fact, in comparison to our need for food and shelter, our social ills are manifold. A hungry stomach can be satisfied with a few potatoes, but a hungry psyche will hardly be contented.

Lack of psychological and economic security breeds group illnesses. Insecurity breeds greed, greed envy, and envy jealousy.

Furthermore, in search of sex, power and a name – even if it is infamy – some of us pre-sell our lives. In the beginning they strive for the 'joy of sex', for wealth and power, but soon the purpose becomes a process which, like a snare, engulfs them. The more they struggle, the greater they thirst. Just like a man eating salted fish, they cannot stop. Their thirst increases, but they can never find satisfaction. The conventional self in Eastern literature is compared with a snake; beautiful on the outside, poisonous inside. It has also been compared to the poppy seed, which produces nostalgia. When the force of the conventional self dominates man, he loses his senses; he pays no heed to truth at all, and submits to any man, woman or thing to satisfy his carnal desire. Even in rational man, if the impulsive self becomes dominant it uses his reason. Such a man becomes a master of 'rationalization'. His impulses dictate the act, but his memory never remembers it. In Sufi literature Satan is known as the first misguided rational and argumentative being.

In a social and historical sense, such a process produces a Hitler, Stalin, Napoleon, Genghiz Khan, or Agha Muhammad Khan (1768–96, Persia) who, after conquering a town which resisted his attack, asked for 2,000 pairs of eyes. When the officer carried out his order, the brutal man sat down and counted them, then turned to the officer and said, 'If two were missing I would have taken yours out'. The power of the conventional self develops in man such a craving that he becomes inhumane. The arts of cunning, guile, and treachery become the rules of success and having security. Such a blind person has lost man's unique quality of discernment and does not differentiate between morality and immorality, false and true, human and inhuman. The more he mistrusts men, the more he fears, and the more he fears, the more power he seeks in order to feel secure:[1]

> Out of his own base needs and state of mind such a man compels everyone to submit to him without question. He expects others to worship him as a leader and god. In the psychological sense such a figure creates idols, which he worships and desires so that even indirectly people will relate themselves to him. Particularly if his own image is somewhat tainted, he also requires people to relate themselves to him by sacrificing and working for his glory.

Those persons who are weak but have a strong conventional impulsive self, become foxy and submit to the powerful. They have no security alone and are always dependent and fearful, finding escape mechanisms and often concealing truth and manipulating others.

An insecure conventional self often develops a miserly and hoarding character. He neither enjoys his possessions nor lets others enjoy them. It is recorded that the aforementioned Agha Muhammad Khan, every night before going to bed, used to scatter the crown jewels on his bed and rub his face against them before he went to sleep. As a child I knew a millionaire who lived alone and ate the cheapest stale bread, often three days old. Everyone pitied him until he died and his millions were discovered. This kind of soul cannot love, and fame and infamy are equal to him.

Further social maladies can appear in terms of general anxiety, fear, injustice and even cruelty towards one another. Hatred, passion, and anger often result from these maladies, which blind people to others' points of view. The result is a failure of social intercourse and a breakdown of communication. Utilizing all these negative tendencies, the person often fails; then there is nothing left except grief and despair.

A large number of other social maladies are caused by man's prejudice, itself the result of provincialism, sectarianism and racism. Every sensible man can learn from his or her own reflection that Moses, Christ and Muhammad arose for the union of men, not for their disunion. Now, contrary to this principle, we can observe the present world and discover that from Canada to Ireland, from the British Isles to Cyprus, from Greece to the heart of Africa, from the Middle East to Asia, from Bangladesh to Taiwan, from Vietnam to the United States and then to Russia, we are dwelling in houses divided against themselves. Social injustices, nationalism, tribalism and prejudice separate people from one another and make men utilize their energy for regression and stagnation.

Still further human malaise results from international historical affairs. History indeed appears as the hysteria of man. Continually, one group has injured another; and when the injured got their chance, they had to take revenge. Their immaturity couldn't guide them to forgive and forget. The Persians set fire to Athens, so the Greeks set fire to Persepolis in the Wars of the Macedonians. The French and later the Germans left Moscow in ashes, so the Russians had to destroy Berlin. After the Germans bombed London continuously, the English had to defend themselves and took revenge. Similarly when the Japanese attacked Pearl Harbour, the United States responded by using the atom bomb. If an impartial judge were to visit the earth, he would find no one innocent. Furthermore, his immediate perception would be that the inhabitants of this beautiful spaceship, earth, are undoubtedly primitive. After seven thousand years of civilization only a handful have seen the mother earth in its true perspective. After centuries of the rise and fall of dynasties, we still fight for territorial boundaries; after successive generations we still possess innumerable languages, without being able to communicate effectively; after centuries of fighting for religious rights we are still irreligious. After centuries of invention, we have easily become the victims, and consider ourselves helpless in the light of our own creations, whether they be machines, economic systems or philosophical ideologies.

Once more 'Attar, the Master Sufi of the twelfth century, encountering similar social maladies during his turbulent time, devoted a whole volume, *The Book of Allah (Allahi Nama)*, to discussing the role of false desires, interests and values which can block the growth of man.

'Attar, in seven thousand lines of beautiful poetry in six sections, discusses the story of a wise man who has six educated sons. All of the sons were successful, but still malcontented. One day the wise father called them in and said, 'If you inform me of your deep desires, I promise to help you to attain satisfaction, or at least to show you the path to happiness.' The sons responded to their father's request, and each one presented his desire as follows:

The first son told the father that he was in love with the daughter of the king of the fairies, and that nothing would make him happy except wedlock with that beloved.

The second son presented his case: he told the father that he was madly in love with magic and sorcery.

The third son wanted to have the crystal ball.

The fourth son was seeking the everlasting spring for an ever-lasting life.

The fifth son was in search of King Solomon's ring.

The sixth son was in love with alchemy.

Hearing them all, the father analysed each case according to its merit. Utilizing various allegorical stories, examples and wise sayings, he showed that their desires were unrealistic and illusory. He then represented the path of Sufi growth to selfhood to them.

The Sufis believed that these fantasies of mind and social ills – namely fear, insecurity, despair, greed, envy, jealousy, passion, carnal love, conceit, anger, deception, lying, miserliness, injustice, even grief and all other individual and social vices – are due to the unhealthy conditions of life. The antithesis to this conventional thesis is religion, and Sufism becomes the synthesis. No one full of the negative forces of conventional self, such as we have described, has a chance to enter the path of the Sufis. Then what should one do? Al-Ghazzali, once in a similar situation, said:[2]

> If we would like to clean the well of the psyche of the polluted rubbish which constantly flows into it by the social currents, we must first stop the flow of such polluted matter and then find a good cleaning detergent and clean the well. Then we must let clean water flow in.

In this respect the real detergent is true religious practice, which can serve as a transitional mechanism to growth to selfhood.

Chapter 3

Religion: a transitional mechanism of growth to selfhood

We have presented the idea of the conventional-impulsive self, its regressive nature, its dimension and its forces which alienate man from his true nature and the reality of human fellowship. In such a condition and at such a time that man becomes a stranger to himself, to nature and to other men, it would behove him to return to a religious conviction, even that of a conventional order. Religious order can thus become a discipline, a mechanism for rebirth. Imagine that someone is drowning in the storm of society and history, and suddenly he discovers a safe cottage where he can stop struggling and can rest, wait and restore his energy and inner and outer power for further exploration. Religion at least can be that safe cottage, though it can become a path to make a Jew an Abraham, a Christian a Christ, and a Muslim a Muhammad. We will later discuss the inherent characterististics of self-renewal in these major religions; that is, after we have developed a concept of what we may call 'religious self' in Islam, which is also applicable to other major religions with some modification.

The greatness of Muhammad was that he said 'I am a man like you, but the instrument of Allah's revelation'. One of his greatest claims, perhaps, was the fact that he didn't claim to have come to give men wealth, knowledge, power, sex or even security. Instead, he claimed: 'I have arisen to complement the human characters and virtues of people.' The significance of this statement increases our wisdom when in the twentieth century we discover that the inhumanity of man to man is not due to wealth, knowledge or power, but is due to his poor virtue and immorality. Now how did Muhammad plan to change people's virtue in a time of total immorality such as our age?

Islam's way to a virtuous life is no different from other religions, though simpler: (1) it makes man aware of his situation; (2) it gives him a conviction, which makes life meaningful; (3) it gives him certain behavioural rules which help to foster inner personal peace and contribute to human fellowship and peace among men; (4) it gives him a personal security; and (5) above all, it gives a purpose to man's life and predicts the continuation of life after physical death. With these simple principles Islam forms the self-image of a Muslim; a character who can continue his self-growth much better than a man who is the slave of his impulses.

With regard to the human situation, the Qur'an, in a small *sura* of three short verses, comprehensively defines it as follows:

> *In the name of God, Most Gracious, Most Merciful:*
> *1 By (the token of) time (through the ages),*
> *2 Verily man is in loss*
> *3 Except such as have faith,*
> *And do righteous deeds,*
> *And (join together)*
> *In the mutual teaching*
> *Of Truth, and of*
> *Patience and constancy.*

In the interpretation of these three verses one can write a volume. It suffices to state here that the greatest capital of each of us is the *duration* (time) which is given to us. This duration is pregnant and potentially rich, and man can utilize it to make the growth that he is endowed with. This capital must be used properly so that 'Adam' becomes *man*, social man a cultured man, and a cultured man a universal man. If we allow impulses and conventional forces to rule in this *opportunity*– our duration, our life – we will be, as the first verse tells us, at loss. The aid to this capital – our time – as the revelation presents, is 'Patience'. We will speak of patience later; here it is enough to say that patience brings harmony and lack of anxiety to our time, to our heart. If we combine the two together, the joyous result appears in terms of growth.

The mechanism of the Islamic self-system thus comes to the aid of our shaky situation. It begins with a conviction and belief in Allah. The believer must understand that there is no Allah (God) but God. Thus, if there are other idols within us, such as attachment to food, to wealth, to sex, to fame, to title, to pride and to sensual art objects, we are not yet Muslims. Furthermore, a Muslim must free himself from attachment to the importance of his family, tribe, nation or race. In this respect Muhammad said: 'A black from Africa and a noble from my own tribe are equal in Islam.' And our Master Rumi said: 'Do not look at his figure and colour, look at his purpose and intention. If he is black [yet] he is in accord with you: call him white, for his complexion is the same as yours' (*Mathnawi*, Book I). Islam rejects blood relationship. Prejudice must disappear from the heart, and one must without reservation say: 'with malice toward none and with charity for all.'

Further idols of the mind must also be uprooted. Even conventional rules of ethics and manners, and conventional ideas of freedom and justice must be changed until no idol remains in the mind and heart. In such an empty heart Allah appears.

In order to change one's previous traditional conduct to Islamic conduct, one must perform every deed for the sake of Allah, in His name and for cultivating His image within the heart and enriching one's faith in Him. In every act one must discover and rediscover Him, again and again, until one feels like a true believer. Thus, the foundation of world-unity is *Tauhid* (Faith in the Unity of All), and in the words of the late M. Iqbal,

> Islam as a policy, is only a practical means of making this principle a living factor in the intellectual and emotional [as well as social] life of mankind. Loyalty to Allah virtually amounts to man's loyalty to his own ideal nature. The ultimate spiritual basis of all life, as conceived by Islam, is eternal and reveals itself in variety of change.

The Prophet's great art of prophecy, therefore, was concerned with Allah, the origin of creation, and the relationship of the physical world and the world of man to a unitary system. He understood the nature of man's conflict and found its resolution only in a new vision. In order to establish this vision he had to analyse and reconstruct the developmental history of past religions and transcend its nature.

In this process he observed man in his naked and helpless state and gave him hope for further growth. Although he accepted the fall of man and his banishment from paradise, he did not stress man's early sin but made life a means of salvation. He took the traditional legend of the fall of man and gave it a new meaning.[1]

> Thus we see that the Quranic legend of the Fall has nothing to do with the first appearance of man on this planet. Its purpose is rather to indicate man's rise from a primitive state of instinctive appetite to the conscious possession of a free self, capable of doubt and disobedience. The Fall does not mean any moral depravity; it is man's transition from simple consciousness to the first flash of self consciousness, a kind of waking from the dream of nature with a throb of personal causality in one's own being. Nor does the Quran regard the earth as a torture-hall where an elementally wicked humanity is imprisoned for an original act of sin. Man's first act of disobedience was also his act of free choice, and that is why, according to Quranic narration, Adam's first transgression was forgiven.

Then, with a superb insight into the potentiality of man, and recognizing that it is only through common positive action that man can unfold himself, Muhammad set up a few simple rules for daily living. He sought to develop peace within the community by establishing a sense for *A'ma* and emphasizing a super-ego for the community so that progress could become possible. In general, the greatness of religion arises from the establishment of this invisible security, which serves as an anchor for the stability of group life and the provision of conditions for further development.

To Muhammad, just as with any other spiritual leader, what was important was action, specifically a unitary action which engaged man's entire organism. Therefore, after establishing the major principles of his religion – viz.: (1) the unitary theory of God; (2) God is just; (3) Muhammad is his prophet; and (4) there is a greater hope for justice by means of a belief in the day of resurrection, in paradise and in the fear of Hell, Muhammad re-emphasized the truth of action, which was an essential tenet of Zoroastrianism and other religions, and which required daily prayer, fasting, the giving of *khoms* (tax of one-fifth of one's income), *zakat* (one-tenth of one's income), pilgrimages, engaging in a holy war if necessary, approving of righteous deeds and disapproving of sinful behaviour. With these few basic rules of social conduct, he created a milieu for comradeship and for brotherhood. Muhammad understood action so well that his insight into its importance even influenced the way of prayer, which requires that the whole organism concentrate on the act of self-suggestion. The manner of prayer affirms the naturalness of life and death, the unity of body and soul, the unity of man and the unity of the external and internal worlds. It gives a symbolic meaning to life as well as strengthening one's character, due to auto-suggestion five times daily. Five times a day every mature person must pray; at dawn, noon, afternoon, sunset and before going to bed. Altogether it takes twenty-four minutes if it is done properly. Part of its simple ritual requires *vozoo* (ablution). The cleanliness which prayer (*nemaz* or *salat*) requires, the good intention which it demands, the understanding which it gives and a living trust in Allah through good deeds are sufficient for keeping well.

Of all Islamic institutions, I believe prayer is the most effective mechanism for self-transformation and the best enemy of undesirable conventional self.

My own definition of prayer is that it is the instrument of detaching one's self from social reality and relating one's self to human destiny. It requires total concentration and a unity of heart, mind and physical expression. Like yoga, it is psychophysical, but better than yoga, it requires preparation, intention and practice. It is the mildest, the simplest and at the same time the most effective experience of well-being.

In the late Sir M. Iqbal's words, 'prayer as a means of spiritual illumination is a normal vital act by which the little island of our personality suddenly discovers its situation in a larger whole of life.'[2]

Prayer in Islam consists of a call to prayer, which helps preparation and includes saying: (1) Allah is the greatest; (2) I testify that there is no God but Allah; (3) I testify that Muhammad is His Prophet (the Qur'an accepts all messengers, from Abraham to Muhammad, as Muslims; that is, those who have made their peace with God); (4) Come to prayer; (5) Come to righteousness; (6) Come to good deeds; (7) Stand in prayer and make intention.

The main portion of the prayer is *Sūra Fatiha*, meaning 'opening', and *Sura Towhid*, meaning 'oneness'. These two short *sūras* comprehensively cover the relation of man to his destiny and illustrate the scope of Islamic Self. The opening *sūra* can be used by any man in any religion; it is universal. This is it:

1 In the name of God, Most Gracious, Most Merciful
2 Praise be to God, the cherisher and sustainer of the worlds;
3 Most Gracious, Most Merciful;
4 Master of the Day of Judgment.
5 Thee do we worship, and Thine aid we seek.
6 Show us the straight way,
7 The way of those on whom
   Thou hast bestowed Thy Grace,
   Those whose (portion)
   Is not wrath,
   And who go not astray.

It is intersting that such a prayer is the beginning of the Qur'an. In its interpretation, authorities believe that though God doesn't need our praise, if it comes from our innermost being it brings us into union with God's will. Then our senses feel good, at peace and in harmony. Evil and conflict disappear, and conventional forces cease to act on us. Social, negative forces and our impulsive needs cannot influence the course of our conduct, for our insight is lifted above them in praise. This leads us to the attributes of God and to the attitude of worship and acknowledgment, and finally brings us to prayer for guidance and a contemplation of what guidance means.

In *Sūra Towhid*, we are given the most comprehensive definition of Allah, representing the ultimate ground of all creative experiences. The Qur'an describes Allah as follows:

> *Say: Allah is one*
> *All things depend on Him,*
> *He begetteth not, and He is not begotten;*
> *And there is none like unto Him.*

Furthermore, although God is identified by numerous names, Sufis prefer to identify Him with 'Light' (essence of creation in modern physics) and creative truth. Light is the essence of creation, and we will discuss it further in a later chapter; here it suffices to point out that the concept of Allah as God is a great means of expanding consciousness. Like an onion, each layer leads us to the core, where we finally see the 'nothingness' which has caused everythingness, the void which has held in a beautiful cone the layers of the onion.

The object of daily prayer is not only relation with the Creator, but also with fellow men. Though one can pray quietly in solitude, the aim of prayer is better achieved in congregation. Therefore, though it is not obligatory to pray in congregation daily, special prayer is designated for Friday (the Muslim's holy day), and it is considered essential for human fellowship. As there is no rank in the rank of prayers, a janitor may stand next to the ruler's son and pray. It further provides an association for spiritual illumination of all. The institution of *Haj* (pilgrimage) furthers this aim and brings the brotherhood of mankind into focus. One can then see the double objectives of prayer; that is, peace within and peace with one's fellow men. In the words of Sir M. Iqbal, the Islamic institution of prayer enlarges the sphere of human association and exemplifies man's inner yearning for his self in the universe:[3]

> Prayer, then, whether individual or associative, is an expression
> of man's inner yearning for a response in the awful silence of the
> universe. It is a unique process of discovery whereby the
> searching ego affirms itself in the very moment of self-negation,
> and thus discovers its own worth and justification as a dynamic
> factor in the life of the universe.

Living by the institution of prayer sincerely, brought gradual
personality changes. However, as a complementary mechanism
to the believer, Muhammad also established the practice of
fasting. Each year, one month (*Ramazan*) was to be devoted to
this task – a practice which again can be interpreted as a
preventive measure for strengthening one's character, becoming aware of the needy and contributing to social welfare.
Furthermore, fasting not only requires physical hunger, but a
healthy social conduct and the utilization of tongue and words
for expressing good thoughts. It gives Muslims an opportunity
to demonstrate good feelings towards one another and to adopt
moderation and self-control. It is also a process of losing weight
and conditioning one's self to improve physical health and
spiritual sensitivity. Abstinence becomes half of the moral and
physical cure. Yet in order to further the communication
between Muslims, to strengthen them on a larger scale and to
provide a greater opportunity for them to share their understanding with one another, Muhammad advocated that pil-
grims go to Mecca, where everyone can meet and a stranger
becomes a brother, in a sense the result of an expanding international super-ego.

To emphasize the communal aspect of Islam, Muhammad
established a pair of corollary principles of individual and
social conduct to prevent the community from losing its stand-
ards, its value system and its orientation. These principles are
the principle of approval and encouragement of what is good
and what is healthy (*amr e be maruf*), and the principle of
disapproval and discouragement of what is unhealthy and
unethical (*nahi e az munkar*). Both of these principles put a
civic duty on any Muslim by demanding just action in the
social scene. They condemn non-involvement and indifference
in situations where one saw a strong, wealthy, but unethical

man oppress a weak, poor or needy person. These principles contradict the indifference and complacency of modern man, as in those instances when a passer-by refuses to assist a woman giving birth to a baby on the sidewalk, or when he ignores the pleas of a woman being attacked. The dynamic force of these two principles gradually developed in every community a pattern of behaviour which was approved by the leading Muslims of that community, and also cultivated a moral authority among the respected personages who acted as mediators in times of need.

To further social justice and eliminate the power of wealth in society, Muhammad, in various verses, insists that the more valuable person in the eyes of God is not the one who possesses abundant wealth, nor the one with great power, but rather the one who is virtuous and the doer of good deeds. Muhammad was so realistic in his evaluation of the power of good deeds in action that he even valued it above prayer, as in the following *Aya*:

> 177: It is not righteousness that ye turn your face to the East and the West; but righteous is he who believeth in Allah and the Last Day and the angels and the Scripture and the prophets; and giveth his wealth, for love of Him, to kinsfolk and to orphans and the needy and the wayfarer and to those who ask, and to set slaves free; and observeth proper worship and payeth the poor-due. And those who keep their treaty when they make one, and the patient in tribulation and adversity and time of stress. Such are those who are sincere. Such are the God-fearing. (*Sūrah* II: The Cow, p. 48).

In order to narrow the differences between rich and poor, Muhammad advocated two more principles of social welfare: *khoms* (one-fifth of one's income) and *zakat* (one-tenth of one's income). Such principles, which are parallel to modern taxation, were to be utilized for the needy and had to be distributed by the respected religious leaders of the community, who became the standard-bearers.

Finally, in times of danger every Muslim must protect his community from destructive factors and must willingly engage in a holy war. Although not many people have taken part in holy wars, the public-spirited function of the Islamic community can be seen in other ways. For centuries, and even today, the pious foundations have been the source of support for educational and religious institutions and hospitals. A good example of such a Muslim was a leading *Mujtehid* in Shiraz after the Second World War. During a severe typhoid outbreak, he organized medical facilities by making doctors available, providing free medicine and even giving coupons for food and daily support to needy families. When the city became short of coal, he provided it with coal. When disruptive political issues arose, he established the 'party of "brethren of light",' which became the most important party in Shiraz. Above all, he set up free early morning and evening courses of classical studies open to all. In the seventh grade, I myself studied Arabic in one of the early morning classes, and by the end of the year I had learned enough Arabic to fulfil my high – school requirements.

When one contemplates further the social rules of Islam, it is surprising to find that Muhammad brought the rule of the market under moral rule. In buying and selling, individuals established a trustful contractual relationship. The ritual of the contract required the utterance of certain phrases in order to complete the transaction. Although such dealings were oral, their significance was that morality and social trust governed the marketing orientation; not the reverse, as is the current economic doctrine.

Finally, Islam gives us faith in the unknown and infinite and emphasizes that this world is like a farmland; one reaps what he cultivates. We now know that the faithful die much easier than others. Is this because of the purity of life? I guess this is true; we observe our deeds and experiences before we depart. If our conventional self is full of injustices, we don't even die easily.

In brief, the Islamic self-image was healthier and more comprehensive than the conventional self, and still is. Sufis used the Islamic self-system as a bridge to Sufism. I might add here that any religious self-system, whether real Christianity, Judaism, Hinduism or Zoroastrianism, is far superior to the present worldly self-system; and each can be utilized as a mechanism of rebirth and transcendence to the Sufi self-system.

A living example of what I have tried to say so far is Muhammad Ali, the heavyweight boxing champion. From Cassius Clay to Muhammad Ali is the distance from the conventional self of the American ghettoes to an Islamic self-image. Muhammad Ali, on various occasions, has explained his self-transformation. From drinking, gambling, stealing and numerous other immoralities of an economic environment, one by chance and at the right moment receives the call of the Islamic self-image. As a result of a change in attitude he adheres to a new lifestyle which is healthier, infinite and positive. In his one interview with Martin Agronsky, one of the leading broadcasting interviewers, Ali tried to explain that upon retiring from boxing, he intends to devote himself to the praise of God and His deeds. The interviewer could not follow Muhammad Ali, and we shouldn't blame him, because he was attached firmly to smoking – a representation of conventional self – and couldn't understand how a man would give up fame and a huge income to devote himself to God. We do understand this decision and in the next chapter will show how *zikr* of Allah could produce a greater self-transformation for Muhammad Ali or any other sincere person.

Chapter 4
From being a Muslim to becoming Allah

We introduced Cassius Clay as a conventional self and Muhammad Ali as a Muslim self-image; the question now becomes: what will Muhammad Ali do now? In his interview with Mr Agronsky he said, 'Man, I would like to devote myself to Allah, to religion.' With this little phrase, though it was difficult for the renowned interviewer to understand the boxer, the champion left an open-ended statement which can be related to infinity. He can apply the simple and comprehensive principles of Islamic faith and create human brotherhood. In fact, since the first two centuries of Islam, a minority of the faithful have tried to do so. However, this is the basic guideline, and though it can have great positive social consequences for the believers, it is not the end of Islam. Practising Islam, studying and reflecting on the meanings of life, experience of the prophets and verses of the Qur'an, will create a new dimension in the life of any Muhammad Ali. Islam considers submission to Quranic discipline the beginning of the believer's inner growth. Every man and woman's duty is to seek understanding of the nature of Allah and revelation. One must seek the knowledge of the true reality beneath rational and irrational faith. The root of imitative faith, rational belief and meditation must be discovered by understanding the nature of revelation and by getting to the proximity of Allah. The actuality of life, and its manifestation, is inherent in Allah. It cannot be realized by conceptualization. It cannot be perceived by the senses or put into words. It can only be felt by a system of higher experience. Sa'di, of the thirteenth century, beautifully describes the image, or the non-image, of Allah:

> *Oh Thou who art beyond logical concepts and imagination,*
> *Oh Thou who art beyond what others have said and*
> *whatever we have studied or heard;*
> *The meeting is now over, this life is at the end, but*
> *We are still at the beginning of defining you.*

(Sa'di, Gulistan)

In other words, no one reaches Allah by thinking, but a devoted and faithful Muslim can relate to Him by purity of intention and by the process of transcendental experience. What does this process of transcendental experience mean? In a sense, it means identification with the image of Allah. Now, the image is so diversified that if one goes even by the holy Qur'an, one finds ninety-nine different nominal descriptions for Allah. For instance, He is the Most Merciful, the Most Compassionate and Soul-creating. He is the Wise, Speech-creating in the tongue, Lord Forgiving and the Most Generous. He is bounteous and without discrimination, and blesses everyone: the criminals, the sinners and the disbelievers as well as the pious, the healthy and the believers. He is the Glorious One, the Life-giving and the Knower of Secrets. He is the Creative Truth, and the Essence of Light. He is the Just and the Judge of all Judges, the Beauty of the Beautiful, and He is what He is.

Now, any Muhammad Ali can spend hours developing each of these attributes within himself, as all true Muslims have done since the Prophet's time. Thus, the second stage in the development of the Muslim self-image is identification with the attributes of Allah. The greatness of all major religions is the fact that images attributed to God are so great and superior that identification with them develops a new man, with God-like attributes. These attributes serve as a transfer for those faithful who seek to transcend the stage of 'name'. Meditation on God's attributes can become a mechanism for harmonizing man's inherently wild qualities which are due to biological processes and historical conflicts. Through meditation on Allah's attributes, a new pattern of behaviour and a rich source of positive attitude are created within the human system, which affect even our physiological expressions. By the process of encounter and assimilation, a conventional-impulsive self will become aware of its inadequacies. After a period of sincere practice of the principles of religion, a believer becomes aware of the attributes of God as a transcendental means. By gradual identification with these attributes, he will further become aware of the ultimate Unity, the One and the All-Allah. Thus Allah becomes a believer's object of desire. He knows that by thinking and analytical discussion he cannot reach Him, but by devotion and *zekr* he can gradually identify with Him. This is a process by which a believer can transform the duality of submission to an authority – even if it is the authority of the Creator – into unity, into becoming God-like. Al-Hallaj, a ninth-century Sufi master, lived at a time such that, after achieving this state of unity, he claimed that he was 'creative truth'. This was the result of identification with God, but his claim was considered a heresy, and al-Hallaj was crucified just as Christ was. Rumi, in the eleventh century, devoted a part of his *Discourses* to discussing the fact that al-Hallaj was a better Muslim than those who submit to God. He beautifully states that saying 'I am creative truth' as a true expression of a Muslim. One who truly makes such a claim has reached the proximity of God. He has eliminated the duality and distance between God and himself. But to claim that 'I am the servant of God' is a lower state of faith, because the servant is still in the state of duality and accepts the distance between himself and his creator as a reality. This symbolizes an immature man, while al-Hallaj had fulfilled his potentiality.

Again, no Sufi master has discussed the object of the Sufi's desire – Allah – and the process of union with Him better than 'Attar. 'Attar devotes one of his books, *The Conference of the Birds (Mantiq ul Tair)*, to this transitional task:[1]

> The soul is hidden in the body, and Thou art hidden in the soul. O Thou who art hidden in that which is hidden, Thou art

more than all. All see themselves in Thee and they see Thee in everything. . . .

O my heart, if you wish to arrive at the beginning of understanding, walk carefully. To each atom there is a different door, and for each atom there is a different way which leads to the mysterious Being of whom I speak. To know oneself one must live a hundred lives.

In *Mantiq ul Tair*, 'Attar takes God as the object of desire and identification. He applies the 'method of Presence' (that is, the assumption that only God is present in every act) so that the seeker ultimately identifies himself with God. Instead of emphasizing that God made man in His image, he helps the seeker to create God in his own image as a mechanism of inner spiritual evolution.

In his allegory, a flock of birds resembling a group of travellers passes through seven purifying stages of inner-evolution travellers pass through seven purifying stages of inner-evolution before finally becoming one with the object of their search – God.

The allegory, after praise of Allah, opens as all the birds (seekers) assemble to seek a worthy leader. The saintly Hoopoe claims he knows the true leader, the legendary God-like Simurgh (Roc), who lives in the mountains of Qaf. Although the place is inaccessible, the Hoopoe willingly offers to guide them there; he explains that life acquires meaning only if one reaches Him.

However, when the Hoopoe describes the difficulties involved in reaching the Simurgh, the other birds find excuses for not undertaking the journey; to each one the Hoopoe points out his error. The ladylike nightingale declares that the rose carries the secret of love. If she is separated from the rose she will surely die; the journey to the Simurgh would overtax her tender strength. The Hoopoe calls her a slave of untrue love. He advises her to seek self-perfection and to forsake the passing love that a rose offers.

The parrot, charming in her green dress of everlastingness, insists that she is seeking the fountain of life, not Simurgh. The Hoopoe tells her to give up her green allure for further growth and a better state of mind.

The pretentious peacock, having sinned and been expelled from paradise, desires only to return there and nothing more. The Hoopoe comments that she has selected the wrong object of desire, for truth dwells in the heart.

The duck, in his holy robes, compulsively performs his ablutions again and again and lacks any desire for the Simurgh. Following him, the self-satisfied partridge is so busy searching for jewels in the mountains that his heart burns from the pebbles that he has greedily swallowed. In reply to him, the Hoopoe states that his love of jewels hardened his heart.

The haughty Homa steps forward boasting that whomever his shadow falls on becomes a king. He smugly asks, 'Does a maker of kings and a giver of thrones need to seek the Simurgh?' The Hoopoe tells him, 'You are a slave of pride satisfied with a bone. Even though you enthrone kings, you will lose their loyalty when misfortune strikes them.'

Like an obedient statesman, the hawk protests, 'Although the king has blinded me, he sets me on his hand and trains me to perform my duties correctly. I'm content with the morsels that I get from his hand. So why should I go to the Simurgh without being called?' The Hoopoe explains that a king's court is like fire, which one must keep away from.

Finally, the heron gives as his excuse his passion for the sea, the owl his desire for the serenity of the ruins, and the sparrow his own feeblemindedness. In answer, the Hoopoe addresses all the birds, 'You indulge in self-pity, identify yourselves with transitory things and have no stake in the things that are enduring. Your close association and argumentativeness leads nowhere. You are all shadows of the Simurgh, but why is it that you have no love for Him? Prostrate yourselves and seek Him. You are perplexed and you can only remedy the situation by striving and searching for the Simurgh, from whom this world came into being.'

The birds finally agree to search for the Simurgh, but before beginning their journey the Hoopoe describes the seven valleys, resembling the Sufi path to perfection, through which they must pass: Quest, Love, Understanding, Independence and

Detachment, Pure Unity, Astonishment and finally Poverty and Nothingness (inner emptiness). The Hoopoe relates that in the Valley of Quest they will encounter situations requiring a great effort to overcome and threatening to distract them from their goal. It may take them several years to succeed in this task. To secure his quest a seeker has to give up all that he possesses. Gradually, the individual devotes himself to the object of his desire. In the final state of quest the seeker finds that nothing matters except the pursuit of his aim. At the end dogma, belief and disbelief all cease to exist.

The Hoopoe tells his listeners that the Valley of Love prepares the seeker for understanding. True love results from perceiving the value of the object of desire. Agitation and distress plague the seeker until he reaches his object. Only through love does inner insight manifest itself and give the seeker strength to identify with the object of desire. Like fire, love knows no afterthought. With the growth of love, good and evil cease to exist; reason and love have nothing to do with one another. A metaphor aptly describes the manifestation of love: upon realizing his origin, the individual becomes like a fish thrown on the beach by the waves, struggling to get back into the water.

The insight gained by love brings one to the Valley of Understanding, a valley which has no beginning or end. One must persist here even though the knowledge one gains is temporary. But here each traveller gains an understanding of the truth according to his own receptiveness. He realizes his potentiality. Although he is not preoccupied with himself, he sees the whole of creation by insight into an atom. As he gradually understands the relatedness of things, he ponders on their secret. Many travellers have lost their way here. One must have an intense desire and longing to become as one ought to be if one is to cross this difficult valley. As one tastes the secret, one will wish to understand it, but must still look for further understanding.

When the seeker gains understanding, he becomes detached and enters the fourth valley, that of Independence. Here he must become independent, materially and spiritually; he must rid himself of the desire to possess and the wish to discover. In this state he feels that the world is negligible, a speck in the universe where nothing new or old has value. One can act or not act, but he must still ponder on the origin of existence.

In the fifth valley, Unity, everything is broken into pieces; everything has lost its temporal and conventional meaning. Ultimately one finds that the evolution of the universe and growth have come from the same source; that is, plurality has sprung from unity. Although the individual may see many forms, they are all one, just as oneness appears in number. Yet he must still seek further, for that which he seeks is beyond unity and number. The eternity of past and future, before and after, vanish as one ceases to speak of them. As the seeker discovers the invisible source of the visible world and the visible becomes nothing, then nothing is left to contemplate.

The Valley of Astonishment follows. In this valley one falls prey to sadness and depression. Sighs become a sword and each breath a bitter sigh. Sorrow, lamentation and a burning eagerness appear. The individual feels completely depressed and despondent, but the one who has already achieved unity forgets all, including himself; he falls into the state of bewilderment. He is now certain he knows nothing, understands nothing, and is unaware of himself, while being in love but without knowing with whom. His heart is both full and empty of love at the same time.

Bewilderment gives way to deprivation, an indescribable state characterized by muteness. In this state the ray of enlightenment dispels the shadows which surround the individual's being. Emerging from this state he will find the secret of creation, and many secrets will be revealed to him. No longer existing separately, he will grasp the beauty of Simurgh, which is hard to hold within him.

Like the Hoopoe, the birds also now yearned for unity. Some died in the excitement of perceiving this unified state. The rest wandered for years and experienced many hardships. Finally, thirty birds (*Si-murgh*) reached their destination. They approached the door of that being who exists beyond human reason and knowledge; they sat there in despair and waited. At last a voice announced that Simurgh would have nothing to do with a group which could only lament. The birds became anxious, but persisted. Now they had passed the final test, the veil of reason of the soul drew completely aside and they discovered that Simurgh, the invisible leader, was themselves, the *Si-murgh* (thirty birds); and that they themselves were the reflection of the essence. At first this discovery of self-transformation, this process of identification with their object of desire, astonished them, for they did not know if they were themselves or if they had actually become Simurgh. But gradually the unity of subject with object and illumination within them persisted. In 'Attar's words: 'And if they looked at both together, both were the Simurgh, neither more nor less. This one was that, and that one this; the like of this hath no one heard in the world.'[2]

So far I have spoken of two types of union, two types of insight. First we mentioned insight into mere faith, and union with its principles, which I call the sphere of 'name' – conventional and imitative belief and culture. Then I discussed a deeper type of union, that of identification with the attributes of God. While consciousness of conventional religious reality brings about illumination of names and the cultural state, identification with attributes eventually causes illumination of qualities. Through the process of illumination of the ordinary religious self one arrives at the state of security of faith without interpretation or insight into its original meaning. Through the illumination of attributes one arrives at self-transformation and development of a new character.

A good example of such change is in the practice of *zikr* (repetition and meditation on Allah). Al-Ghazzali, in *Al Munquaz Men al-Zalal* (*Deliverance from Ignorance*), mentions the condition of *zir*; that is, the *zaker* (mentioner) first must empty himself of all thoughts and emotion. Then he emphasizes that, with total concentration:[3]

Let there be no dichotomy of positive and negative. Then sit alone in a quiet place, free of any task or preoccupation. . . . Let nothing besides God enter the pysche. Once you are seated in this manner, start to pronounce with your tongue, 'Allah, Allah,' keeping your thought on it.

Practice this continuously and without interruption; you will reach a point when the motion of the tongue will cease, and it will appear as if the word just flows from it spontaneously. You go on in this way until every trace of the tongue movement disappears while the heart registers the thought or idea of the word.

Continuing with the invocation, there will come a time when the word will leave the heart completely. Only the palpable essence or reality of the name will remain, binding itself ineluctably to the heart.

Up to this point everything will have been dependent on your own conscious will [see chapter on effort, *kushesh*]; the Divine bliss and enlightenment that may follow have nothing to do with your conscious will or choice. You have laid yourself exposed to what God may breathe upon you, as He has done upon His prophets and saints.

If you follow what is said above, you can be sure that the light of Truth will dawn upon your heart. At first intermittently, like flashes of lightning, it will come and go. Sometimes when it comes back it may stay longer than other times. Sometimes it may stay only briefly.

The key to our next stage, which is identification with the essence, is in the flashes of light. Light, one of the most important names of God, is definitely the source of many elements, perhaps life itself. The illumination of essence, which is hard to explain, occurs spontaneously. It is compared to a sharp sword which cuts the past from the future and lets the Sufi feel the total presence. Through concentration, every intelligent man can remove the 'name' from an object and arrive at a concrete situation, even arrive at the invisible phenomena behind the forces – the fluid composition of the material, the break of the atom – but it is the illumination of the essence which the Sufi master is capable of unfolding, and which relates him at least temporarily to cosmic communication.

Sa'di, with regard to experience of the essence, tells us that one who experiences it gives no news of it. Hafiz, in analysing the situation, tells us that the one (referring to al-Hallaj) who exposed the secret was crucified. We might mention here that

it is recorded that when al-Hallaj was crucified, drops of his blood formed the phrase, 'I am creative truth', right at the place of his crucification and brutal dismemberment. I there-
place of his crucifixion and brutal dismemberment. I there-
only illuminated the Sufi's heart but also caused physiological changes, including changes in chemistry of blood. Unfortunately, unlike the study of physiological changes in human systems of Zen masters in Japan by the late Sato and Professor Akichige, Middle Eastern scientists have not yet explored such changes, but it is definitely a vital subject for possible scientific verification. To me, Sufi masters possessed more sensitive antennae for communication than presently available.

The late Aldous Huxley, who had great interest in mystical experience, in 1962 at the International Congress of Applied Psychology held in Copenhagen, discussed the 'visionary experience' as one of the major characteristics of the fulfilled self. He further explained the experience of illumination and undifferentiated light as a major factor in reaching deep into the essence of creation. He said:[4]

> In general, I think it is possible to say that the experience of undifferentiated light tends to be the experience associated with the full-blown mystical experience. The mystical experience, I think, may be defined in a rather simple way as the experience in which the subject relationship is transcended and in which there is a sense of complete solidarity of the general with other human beings, and with the universe in general.

In modern science, the essence of light which Sufis sought can be visualized as the 'mother element', that which makes all known elements possible.

The result of union with essence will be the experience of *An*. This subject is the heart of Sufi experience, and we have devoted the last chapter to it; here it suffices to say that the psychological mechanism of Sufism should be found in the process of identification, and its product in the climax of the experience of our being. While the process was universal, the object of identification varied. It was variety of object of desire which produced hierarchy of personalities.

In the eighth century A.D., the Sufis chose their object of identification from among the attributes of the Prophet and God. Sufism in this respect was identical with virtuous man. As respected community members, Sufis participated in the social life and lived simply; some practised asceticism, perhaps due to association with Christian brothers. At the end of that century, social conditions fostered the spread of asceticism; its most outstanding proponent was Ebrahim Ibn Adham (d. A.D. 777), a prince from Balkh, who experienced a situation similar to that of Buddha. Upon receiving his call, Adham forsook his conventional self to search for inner enlightenment and growth to selfhood. He earned his living by gardening. In present-day Iraq and north-east Iran Adham's followers perfected the process of Sufism. Some of the most important advocates of this school withdrew from society.

In the ninth century A.D., the Sufis made Baghdad their centre. They gradually came to believe that God Himself, as we discussed previously, can become the Sufi's object of desire. Not only did this process of Sufism become a form of personality change, but it also developed into an institutionalized hierarchy which made growth to selfhood through identification with representatives of God easier and possible. Thus it is necessary that we discuss the process and hierarchy of Sufi personality in the next few chapters; but before we end this chapter it would be just and appropriate to mention that rebirth through God's image was not unique in Islam. Other religions also shared the idea. For instance, the late Thomas Merton, who corresponded with me for several years, believed that self-renewal is one of the basic characteristics of Christianity. Contrary to the belief which makes it seem that Christianity is a formalistic method for gaining a place in this world, Merton believed that the death of 'old self' will create a new dimension in one's present life, to say nothing of salvation.

In the theology of the New Testament, Merton maintained that self-renewal is the product of an inner evolution which

> in its ultimate and most radical significance implies complete self-transcendence and transcendence of the norms and

attitudes of any given culture, any merely human society. This includes transcendence even of religious practices. The whole sense of Paul's polemic with Judaism, a theology of grace which has had a decisive effect in shaping Western culture, lies in his contention that the Christian who has attained a radical experience of liberty 'in the spirit' is no longer 'under the law.' He is henceforth superior to the laws and norms of any religious society, since he is bound by the higher law of *love*, which is his freedom itself, directed not merely to the fulfillment of his own will but rather to the transcendent and mysterious purposes of the spirit: i.e. the good of man. [personal writing to the author]

Any Sufi would go along with this statement of Merton's, and in response to his writing I wrote:

In order that we achieve the state of selfhood, we must be born twice; once physically and another time psychologically. The process of psychological birth includes several rebirths which include an inner call, a conscious effort known as *kushesh*, and an effortless happening known as *keshesh* – attraction.

Chapter 5

The rise of the inner voice and the moment of resolution

Several years ago, on a Monday morning, a medical student came to visit me. He was anxious and in despair. He told me that for years he had imitatively been religious and had followed his parents regularly to church. He did this customarily and was unconscious of it. However, the Sunday before he visited me was different. He had suddenly noticed a change; he had beome self-conscious and had developed doubt in his regular Sunday religious ceremony as it was conducted in their church. He had not discussed his doubts with anyone, but had experienced a release and an agony the night before he visited me. We discussed the nature of his parental belief as well as the nature of his sudden disbelief. As he was an understanding individual, we gradually came to the conclusion that his sudden awareness could provide a great opportunity for him. He could become a deist, that is, apply his reason to his belief and accept it; or he could analyse the origin of Christianity and become Christ-like or even become experientially religious. He decided that he would explore the nature of deism, and hopefully because of his background it gave him a great satisfaction. It went along with his scientific interest. He parted with greater satisfaction than when he came to visit me. The moment of awareness and a new conviction was ripe, and his sincerity made a way for him. It was a gift that the Church had offered him. For years, though he had gone to church customarily, he had not questioned it and he hadn't outgrown the imitative religious ceremony. Now, being more rational, he was seeking a deeper reason to support his belief, and this had a tradition in deism which he could understand and enjoy. It is in the light of such experience that the religious renewal of President Carter is easy for us to understand but for some commentators, difficult to believe in. Did President Carter experience a similar awareness to that of our medical student? I assume so, and we hear that he then re-examined his belief and renewed his religious conviction for the better.

Is it possible that one day in the future our medical student will arrive at the end of deism and discover that if there is a God, He must be beyond conceptualization? What will he do then? Al-Ghazzali, a renowned philosopher (d. 1111), experienced such a situation at a time of existential doubt, and his experience, and later his moment of conviction to Sufi reality, is a good example of such a human situation. Al-Ghazzali was not at the beginning of rational self, but at its end. Therefore his struggle was massive because, while our medical student had very little to lose, al-Ghazzali had to renounce his own philosophical writings, fame and a comfortable life.

Separation from all he had worked for for many years was not an easy task, even under pressure of a strong avocation. To get acquainted with the nature of his malady we had better turn to his own words, in his *Confession*.

In talking to the readers of his *Confession*, al-Ghazzali relates his experience as follows:[1]

> [That you may] ... wish to know my experiences while disentangling truth lost in the medley of sects and divergencies of thought, and how I have dared to climb from the low levels of traditional belief to the topmost summit of assurance.

He further tells us of all his philosophical and religious studies and relates to us that 'children are born according to creation but their parents make them Jews, Christians or Muslims'. Trying to free himself from hereditary belief, and fetters of tradition and borrowed theories of schools of philosophies, in his early thirties he received his inner voice. In search of truth and certainty, he re-examined sense perception, and found that it couldn't be trusted. Then he examined intellectual notions and like Rumi discovered that in the existential sphere they are inadequate, or in Rumi's words, 'The legs of logicians are wooden; and wooden legs are not trustworthy.' In short, intellect at its best produces a Faust, a Satan and a Hamlet. Though they give us argumentation, they never actualize the meaning of life. However, he realized that if intellect matures, and if assumptions of intellectual notions are analysed, man may discover a new power, which he calls intuition and believes manifests itself when, under certain conditions, all senses merge into a union. Noticing the signs and power of this new faculty in the Sufis, he turned to Sufism for help because, although he had concluded that theology had healing power for some, he did not find it a remedy for his own malady.

He acquired a thorough knowledge of Sufism but discovered that he still was prey to uncertainty. Further examination of his own inner voice and his outer status finally convinced him that Sufism consists of experiences rather than of definitions, instruction and conceptualization. So his moment of conviction came at last. After two months of struggle with himself, he left his seat and devoted himself to the practice of Sufism; but it is instructive to present al-Ghazzali's inner state of uncertainty, just before the moment of his conviction to Sufism. He describes his last struggle thus:[2]

> One day I decided to leave Baghdad and to give up everything; the next day I gave up my resolution. I advanced one step and immediately relapsed. In the morning I was sincerely resolved only to occupy myself with the future life; in the evening a crowd of carnal thoughts assailed and dispersed my resolutions. On the one side the world kept me bound to my post in the chains of covetousness, on the other side the voice of religion [the inner voice] cried to me, 'Up! Up! Thy life is nearing its end, and thou hast a long journey to make. All the pretended knowledge is nought but falsehood and fantasy. If thou dost not think now of thy salvation [growth], when wilt thou think of it? If thou dost not break thy chains today, when wilt thou break them?' Then my resolve was strengthened; I wished to give up all and flee; but the Tempter, returning to the attack, said, 'You are suffering from a transitory feeling, don't give way to it, for it will soon pass. If you obey it, if you give up this fine position, this honourable post exempt from trouble and rivalry, this seat of authority safe from attack, you will regret it later on without being able to recover it.'

Thus I remained torn assunder by the opposite forces of earthly passions and religious aspirations, for about six months from the month of Rajah of the year A.D. 1096. At the close of them I yielded and I gave myself up to destiny. God caused an impediment to chain my tongue and prevented me from lecturing. Vainly I desired, in the interest of my pupils, to go on with my teaching, but my mouth became dumb. The silence to which I was condemned cast me into a violent despair; my stomach became weak, I lost all appetite; I could neither swallow a morsel of bread nor drink a drop of water.

The enfeeblement of my physical powers was such that the doctors, despairing of saving me, said, 'The mischief is in the heart, and has communicated itself to the whole organism; there is no hope unless the cause of his grievous sadness be arrested.'

The diagnosis was correct; the root of al-Ghazzali's malady was rejection of his own call for the next stage of consciousness. In the end he acted courageously and detached himself from his esteemed position, honour, wealth, and family. He retained only enough income for a pious living and for the support of his family. He adopted 'intentional isolation' and devoted himself to his own self-transformation and to experiencing the art of rebirth as advocated by Sufism. He travelled in the Middle East from Syria to Mecca and finally, after his rebirth in Khorasan, he was reunited with his family. There in Khorasan he lived creatively for the rest of his life. His process of rebirth encompassed ten years. In his own words,[3]

During my successive periods of meditation there were revealed to me things impossible to recount. All that I shall say for the edification of the reader is this: I learned from a sure source that the Sufis are the pioneers on the path of God; that there is nothing more beautiful than their life, nor more praiseworthy than their rule of conduct, nor purer than their morality. The intelligence of thinkers, the wisdom of philosophers, the knowledge of the most learned doctors of the law would in vain combine their efforts in order to modify or improve their doctrine and morals; it would be impossible. With the Sufis, repose and movement, exterior or interior, are illuminated with the light which proceeds from the Central Radiance of Inspiration.

In the life of Jalalalddin Rumi the moment of conviction arrived also at the height of his fame and social greatness.

Though he had knowledge of Sufism and had learned it through a student of his father – Burhan al-Din Tirmidi, by then a well-known Sufi in Khorasan – he still was not satisfied. In fact, through several years of experience in teaching he had realized that knowledge alone does not change man, nor does instruction greatly help man's growth to selfhood. Fully conscious of the unity of experience, he became concerned about the source of conflict between Muslim sects and those of Jews, Christians, Zoroastrians and others. Observing these superficial divergencies, he then complained openly that every one of the seventy-two religious sects was unaware of the others' states:[4] 'the Sunni is unaware of the Jabri (determinists), the latter is unaffected by the Sunni; they have opposite ways. The Jabri says that the Sunni is lost, the latter asks, what awareness does the Jabri have?'

Under such a mature and critical state of mind, and after actualization of the parental superego and achievement of fame, he met Shams of Tabriz (a Sufi master), who kindled his inner voice and caused Rumi to re-examine his life and seek the true cosmic experience, and to reflect on the experience of revelation and then contemplate on Quranic verses.

To Rumi, Shams was an unfolding of mankind in the memory of the universe in evolution. His illuminating influence made Rumi follow his inner voice and arrive at the moment of conviction. This moment of a new course for growth to selfhood was so precious to Rumi that even though one of his sons was killed in a riot against Shams, he didn't return to conventional fame.

The moment of conviction sometimes arrived at an earlier age. In the case of Abu Yazid Bastami (d. 874), 'the moment', as 'Attar records in his memorable book *Tadhkirat al-Auliya* (*Muslim Saints and Mystics*), 'came very early'. One day Abu Yazid, while studying the Qur'an, came to the verse: 'Be thankful to *Me*, and thy parents.' These words moved him deeply. He left school and hurried home. 'Why have you come home?' cried his mother. Abu Yazid explained that he had reached the verse where God commands him to serve her and Him both. With one heart 'I cannot have two beloveds; with one mind I cannot manage two households. Either you request me from God so that I serve you, or resign me to God so that I dwell wholly with Him.' His wise mother resigned Abu Yazid to God. He in return took the challenge at the right moment and devoted himself to Allah for thirty years, after which he would claim: 'For thirty years God was my mirror, I am now my own mirror.' Such a certain identification with the essence of creation is indeed rare, even in the history of Sufism.

Our next case is Prince Ebrahim Ibn Adham of Balkh (d. 782). Adham lived gloriously in Balkh, as did Buddha centuries before him. His family for generations had practised lordship; he found it a headache. Thus, at the right time he responded to his inner voice and to symbolism which appeared in his dreams and the visions which he saw during the day. As a result, he was convinced that the time for transcendence of social consciousness and entrance into cosmic consciousness had arrived. He entered the path and continued until he became one of the illustrious Sufi masters.

Beshr ibn al-Hareth (d. 841) was at heart a good man but could not give up drinking parties. After a number of years his inner condition was revealed to a saint of Baghdad, who visited Beshr at a wine party; and there he told him that he had a message from Allah for him. The hint was enough for Beshr, who bid goodbye to his friend and entered the Sufi path. A man like Cassius Clay became a sage.

Shaqiq of Balkh (martyred in 810) was a well-known merchant whose conversations with an idol-worshipper, a Zoroastrian and a slave made him make his resolution.

There are many other examples, and I believe that most people at least once in their lives have heard their voice and often overlook its significance, as the flock of birds did to the call of the Hoopoe. However, many others, including thieves, princes, soldiers, slaves, merchants, weavers, goldsmiths, coppersmiths, shoemakers, sweepers and housewives, religious leaders, lawyers, teachers, writers, poets, physicians, mathematicians, shopkeepers and farmers have responded to the call of their inner voice. Some, at the right time, were in a holistic situation which helped them to make their conviction. At such a moment their awakened hearts overruled the demand of their impulses and they rejected the argumentation of mind. This transcendental moment is superior to the moment of repentance (*Tūba*), but shares the same characteristics. Repentance is the moment of weaning oneself from sin, but the moment of conviction is the time of weaning oneself from concepts of good and bad, and of realization of the fact that good and bad are cultural products. The moment of acquaintance with one's own superior consciousness is the moment of one's vow with the reality of revelation and inspiration. It will direct the novice to the reality of immortality and closeness to creative essence – God. However, we must understand that its occurrence is spontaneous. It cannot be produced by knowing, by instruction or by forcing oneself to it. It only comes when unity and harmony of our system have been achieved. It is a moment when our pair of physical eyes, through purity of soul, transform themselves to the unity of an inner eye.

A number of factors may nurture this transformation. For example, sincere recitation of holy verses may suddenly turn the reader to identify himself with the moment of revelation of those verses and make them more valuable than mere recitation. Such a situation, like an intentional discovery in a laboratory, produces a greater courage for a quest. An occurrence of illumination of higher consciousness is self-directing and self-expanding, and it can carry the body along with it. The experiential moment of life unifies our faculties and creates what Ibn al-Arabi, al-Ghazzali and others have termed 'heart'. Heart thus is a faculty for the direct path to illumination, and when it is active we are all 'eyes', or all 'ears', or all 'silence', with a magnetic sense of communication. At that moment we are all receiver or all giver, and while devoid of thought and intelligence, we are all aware.

Discovery of this new medium of communication with the non-human and the human environments creates a longing and a direction; the longing appears because for the first time, one experiences the multi-realities of the environment. One senses the state of the solid and physical, the state of qualities and fluid and the state of essence in astral codes of waves and signals. The awakened man is suddenly concerned with the soul of the object and then with the Soul of Souls of all objects, but he also senses that he is separated from that joyous essence. The weak fade away and the strong take the 'courage to be' as a challenge. In the process of this experience the painful sense of effort passes away, and the joy of contemplation takes possession of the mind. Like a faithful dog he stands on guard. He waits for the gift to arrive. He learns by experience that he must remain steady and sensitive. He must wait and tune up his system so that a flash of truth illuminates the psyche. A few even short experiences convince him that he must be delivered from himself. In every experience his heart is attracted to a single object of desire. Tranquillity, totality, happiness and the union of subject and object appear, because the individual has forsaken all else and is wholly engrossed in the contemplation of the one unique object of desire. In such moments it seems that vertical growth ceases, and the infinite universe expands beyond. However, he feels that he is dwelling in the truth, that he is genuine, and he ceases to act partially. He experiences only according to his capacity, the limit of his insight, and the strength of his resolution.

Now having seen the end in the mirror of the beginning, he would like to increase his capacity, to improve the sincerity of his resolution. He is still not in control of his psyche, but he has his conviction that he is thirsty enough to enter on the Sufi path; the art of purification for experiencing the actuality of life instead of knowing or hearing about it. In this process our *salik*, the novice, may notice the signs in the guide's expression or may receive a hint from a situation and discover that he must devote himself to purification of his own soul and activate his 'heart' as the Chinese artists did. The story is narrated that at one time a group of Greek and Chinese artists were competing with each other at a court. The king, a patron of art, put them to a test. He housed them in separate rooms with door facing door, and told them to create their finest work of art. The Greeks requested all kinds of paints, while the Chinese asked for nothing except tools with which to remove the rust and discolouration from the walls. After some time, the king visited the artists. When the Greeks drew aside the curtain the king saw a picture, so beautiful that it robbed him of his wits. When he entered the room of the Chinese they drew aside their curtain; the reflection of the Greek painting on their highly polished wall was so overwhelmingly beautiful that it robbed him of his sight. The polished wall is the heart of the Sufi which illuminates whatever is in the creation. The Greeks were still intellectual and rational in their work. They were self-conscious. The Chinese here are the symbol of cosmic consciousness; representative of man's pure heart which grasps truth spontaneously and so quickly that interpretation and search are not needed. Rumi says: 'When the psyche is in darkness one needs the light of reason to see his way through life, but when the psyche is illuminated no one needs reason's candle.'

Now the moment has arrived, the *salik* has heard the inner voice. He has taken his vow and he would like to polish the heart. What should he do? The Sufi system has devised two mechanisms for such an inner growth: (1) *kushesh* (devoted effort); (2) *keshesh* (spontaneous attraction and illumination). Though the moment of decision-making was a gift and one had to wait for it effortlessly, the mechanism of *kushesh* requires intentional effort because it deals with re-examination of one's attitude, conduct and behaviour. In contrast, the mechanism of attraction and illumination is the result of grace, and like the initial moment is due to a ripening of the inner and outer condition. The next two chapters will deal with these two mechanisms of progress in the path to selfhood. I consider the moment of initial resolution to be half of the task, the mastery of these two mechanisms the other half of the growth to selfhood, which leads to the 'climax of human being', our conclusion.

Chapter 6

The dual mechanism of the Sufi path

Stages of personality change

Introduction

The moment of conviction, taking a vow and making a resolution to go through the path of the Sufis for growth to selfhood, is like a good question which provides half of the answer. However, the early flashes of the path are just like a gate which opens to a garden of peace and abundance of blessings. After our resolution, it is easy to enter the garden, but reading the signs, making the right turn, are not so easy. There may come a period of ambivalence at every turn. One may feel intense anxiety of separation as well as anxiety of union to come. One may misjudge one's own ability, or fail to realize the difficulties ahead. I once said, 'Search is like love, easy to enter but difficult to fulfil or get out.' In such a state one may regress or strive alone to overcome the difficulty of the path. But the struggle may be fruitless. In such a state the question arises: What should a devoted seeker (*salik*) do in order to make the journey safely, complete his inner evolution and arrive at the final state of selfhood without great hardship?

Certainly, he should realize that his courage is not enough, that is, he may enter the path alone, but during the long journey in struggling out of the dark inner abyss and unknown territory, he will need a guide (a *dalil-e-rah*), a light of the way, and above all he will need a protected environment, a way from daily obstacles in order to purify himself and recapture life. Thus, after a long physical search, the seeker will arrive at a *khanega* (ashram) to begin the period of intentional isolation. He will start by changing clothes and putting on the robes of undyed wool in order to symbolize his intention. The unique qualities of *suf* (undyed wool) are even now not fully under-stood, although the youth movement in the US has adopted simple clothing, often made of natural fibres, comparable to that of the Sufis. Moreover, the early Christians adopted similar robes, and early Muslims dyed their beards as a way of recognizing one another.

The simplicity of wool, its naturalness, warmth, and utility were qualities which aptly suited the physical and spiritual needs of the novice Sufis. In fact, some believe that the term 'Sufi' is derived from *suf* (wool). Later on, patched cloaks or highly decorated robes (*khirqa*) replaced the rough woven wool robes; if the robe had been owned by a *pir*, a renowned guide of a spiritual order, it acquired great symbolic value for the recipient. Furthermore, the kind of *khirqa* worn revealed the order to which the Sufi belonged, his spiritually attained state, the authority, and even the degree of gratification and self-illumination he had attained. In our contemporary world, the American president customarily uses several pens to sign an important document and then distributes the pens. Likewise, on the day of convocation the university graduates put on their symbolic robes in order to receive diplomas. A monarch may bestow knighthood or special recognition to those who have distinguished themselves in his service. So too a Sufi, after a life of experiential spiritualism, received a *khirqa*, which he often valued more than his own life.

By wearing the wool robe, the novice showed his intention of readiness to leave the world of *zaher* (social reality) and submit himself to the world of *batin* (inner reality). In other words, after entering the path of Sufism, the seeker isolated himself in order to reduce the pressures of the 'world of many' (*kathrat*) and concentrate on the world of essence (*wahdat*). The world of unity, the essence of all life (*towhid*), was final attainment for any Sufi. In fact, Abu Said, the Master Sufi (d. A.D. 1049) summarized the whole process of rebirth in totality thus: 'Sufism consists of two steps: taking one step out of one's self and taking another step into God.' Tagore, a remarkable man of the twentieth century, was able to explain the world of 'unity in diversity' as a state of psyche where the personal self tries to reach the limit of the cosmic self. Rumi broadened both these views; he defined the mechanism of Sufism in terms of *fana* (disintegration of the negatives), and *baqa* (reintegration into the positive waves of life). In fact, Rumi did not believe that reintegration of the positive was possible without disintegration of the negative forces which govern man. In *Diwan e Shams*, he beautifully summarizes this point of view: 'Unless you are first disintegrated, how can I reintegrate you?' Here disintegration refers to the passing away of the conventional self, reintegration means rebirth into man's totality. *Fana*, the disintegration of obstacles, is removal of the small 'i', *baqa* is the ascendance of the real 'I'. Instead of being related to a limited socio-intellectual consciousness, *baqa* is the process of becoming a totally conscious being. In a practical sense, *baqa* means cleansing one's own consciousness of fictions, idols, and untruths, and purifying the heart of intense envy, jealousy, grief, and anger so that the spirit regains its original quality of becoming mirror-like to reflect the reality within it. *Fana*, in other words, means liberation from the phenomenal self, and *baqa* is the manifestation of natural life. Again, Rumi beautifully captures this mood: 'Oh, happy is the man who was freed from himself and united with the existence of the living One.'

Though these two processes, unlearning and reliving, make up the essence of self-transformation, a slow deliberation is required, particularly a great deal of effort and conscientious striving aided by blessing, grace, and guidance. To facilitate the act of self-liberation for the actualization of cosmic self, Sufism, in its long history and tradition, has developed elaborate procedures and stages of inner evolution. The depth and breadth of the Sufi path of rebirth is comprehensive, and the more one becomes aware of it the better one appreciates the depth of understanding of the human psyche. Its mechanism, unlike Western psychological thinking, is not based on 'knowing', but transcendental character and inspiration. In fact, a study of Sufi cases would reveal that it was often the realization of the uselessness of 'knowing' in the realm of existence which led prominent philosophers and scientists to enter the path. The Sufi path is a dual way which covers both the refinement of man's external (behaviouristic) nature and his internal (meditative) quality. Its path is like a coin which has two sides, or a reversible jacket. The external aspect of the Sufi path establishes, as we shall explain, stages for strengthening the seeker's faith in what he is seeking, as well as removing the mental blocks and unlearning unsuitable behaviour and purifying his soul. Likewise, the inner way has designated stages and *ahwal,* that is, inner states of the psyche which prepare the individual for experiencing illumination. Prayer, meditation, and inner observation are all essential for the process of inner evolution. However, the principle of individual uniqueness applies here. Each seeker's situation differs, depending on his previous experience. An ethical man has less difficulty in going through the process of Sufism than one who has had a lack of concern for purity of action. The former has a touchstone and is closer to human naturalness; thus, he may spend a shorter period in actualization of the purity of soul than the latter. On the other hand, a man who has distorted his own feelings and has been disputive and argumentative in his actions will experience more strain in liberating himself from previous obstacles than one who has lived harmoniously.

Purity in action is the essence of Sufism and without it no revelation (illumination) takes place. Straightforwardness is both a by-product and an essential prerequisite for the Sufi way. Initially, each seeker must leave the world of 'to have', then make his intention and release himself from the pressure of wealth and possession, but the removal of emotional and mental blocks will not be as easy, for it requires years of conscious effort (*kushesh*) and years of experience through perseverance and grace (*keshesh*) so that *An* happens, and creative flashes occur in the psyche.

Kushesh: the will to behavioural transformation

When the urge for rebirth occurred, the seeker found himself moving away from social reality, and if courageous, he sought the protective environment of the *khaneqa*, where he accepted the guidance of a selected guide, and submitted himself to intentional isolation. The novice had now accepted the challenge and courageously adopted intentional isolation at a time when he had only a faint glimmer of his ultimate goal, that is he could visualize it through its personification, the guide. While images in the holy book (Qur'an) and life histories of Muslim saints provided some comfort to an isolated soul, they were of secondary importance. The seeker gradually had to discover every psychic stage, and this required a re-examination of the conventional self, a product of man's biological evolution, plus the offshoots of this biological energy evidenced in dogmatic child-rearing, socialization, professional specialization, and conventional ways of life. The re-examination of this aspect of life required intense conscious effort (*kushesh*), characterized by strong discipline, constant identification, and transformation of undesirable values, interests, behaviours, thoughts, words, and deeds. Undesirable here refers to whatever hinders the seeker's progress. Every worthless concept which the individual had received through education, instruction, and even Aristotelian logic had to be re-examined. From a modern point of view the stages of ego development parallel the growth of the conventional self of past generations, with one exception: the conventional self (that is, the ego) of contemporary man is more complex and requires a greater effort to be eliminated or at least minimized and transformed into intuitive wisdom. In the past, a strong super-ego dominated a very weak ego (rational ability); today a very complex ego structure is intertwined with animal instincts, thereby promoting a destructive force.

Even though the power of reason in modern man is gradually weakening, enlightened activists, such as genuine scientists, legal authorities, some intellectuals, and above all, psychologists and clinicians, still try to help their clients objectify social reality, cope with it, become reasonable in their dealings with others, and manage their everyday affairs. Many individuals go to a specialist for years in the hope that he will cure their present dissatisfaction and anxiety by rationally examining their past. Sociologists, anthropologists, politicians, and philosophers have become craftsmen in treating such maladies. However, in trying to merge the personal self with the collective self, a greater conflict may arise, adversely affecting both the individual and his group. At a much deeper level the Sufi order tried to untie the cord of the social self, experiencing even greater spiritual transcendence. I am totally convinced that the Sufi approach to removing the culturally dominant images in order to bring forth the real self was a more lasting and meaningful treatment than present-day analysis as pursued by technical specialists. For this reason it deserves a thorough examination here.

In his solitude, the Sufi novice generally began by examining himself in terms of his aim while realizing that most of the elements of his social self were more fiction than real, and he tried to comprehend what it meant to be a Sufi, perhaps pondering on the ideas of the great Baghdad Sufi, Al-Junayd (d. 910), who had written: 'die to one's self (the bio-social self) and live in God'. Or he might study Abu Said who had said: 'To be a Sufi means to erase the source of all worries', and 'no worry is greater than one's bio-social self'. People then as now were over-occupied with their worldly selves; they could not perceive reality. They were separated from God, from the true object outside of their own self, and thus they had to step out of their own self trap and enter into Him. Another Master Sufi, Shehab-edin Suhravardi also had words of advice: 'Sufism is the art of relating to the Creator through purest love (*mehr*) and by means of absolution in Him. *Mehr* is a mechanism stronger than the love between lover and beloved and purer than sexual love.'

In attempting to apply these images, the Sufi found that the first step was to forgive all those whom he felt had wronged him. 'Forgive thy enemy' became a stronger spiritual directive than thinking and preparing for revenge. To Sufis, revenge was a waste of time and a source of human regression, while forgiveness was a powerful means of attaining purification. Sufis valued forgiveness more than intellect, laws, and even such religious tenets as 'an eye for an eye; a tooth for a tooth'. The seeker recognized that he was responsible not only for the act of forgiveness but for the cultivation of the idea within his heart, a more difficult process. His feelings and emotions had to support the idea – otherwise it would not become a part of his character. He therefore spent his solitude in transforming his ideas into feelings and cultivating those feelings. It was not unusual for him to search out the wrong-doer, serve him, and demonstrate genuine kindness, until both he and the Sufi were embued with a feeling of compassion. Historically, there were situations where the Sufis' act of forgiveness actually led rivals or wrong-doers to kneel and kiss the hand of the seeker and seek his pardon.

Thus, this humane way of resolving conflict proceeded by removing dislike and hatred, and strengthening the trust between men, not by matching physical power with power, not by face to face confrontation, not by acquiescing in the wrong-doer's wishes and aims, but by forgiving the causes of the wrong deeds and by strengthening the psyche and demonstrating a more humane character. In other words, one does not have to suffer, run away or bear the consequences, but only cast off those superfluous masks so as to liberate oneself and follow the path of inner evolution.

The Sufi seeker thus begins with the easy course of behavioural transformation. Forgiveness is easy when compared with later stages. No matter how difficult forgiveness might be for the seeker, it was an act over which he had total authority; the will to forgive was his. If he found it hard to act in this manner, he could strengthen his conviction by reciting examples, verses from the Qur'an, and by concentrating on the image he would like to become, by prayer and by symbolic communication from his guide (*pir*).

The second half of this developmental stage (*tawba*), repentance, required even greater courage than the first. While forgiveness of one's enemy or wrong-doer was totally one's own business, repentance was basically attained by the grace of God. The seeker knew that he had done a great deal of wrong, if not to others, at least to himself, for that related to the purpose of his being there. He recognized that he had often sacrificed the end for the means. Thus, the extension of this stage depended on the experience and the state of the Sufi seekers. However, whatever the complexity of wrong-doings or sins of the previous stage, the Sufi had great faith in the grace of God. Sufis often strengthened their faith as seekers by chanting; novices often recited in the midst of darkness and isolation such verses in the name of God as:[1]

> Come back, come back, wherever you are,
> Come back.
> If you are idol-worshipper, Zoroastrian, or
> idolater, come back;
> This court of ours is not a court of despair;
> If you have broken the covenant for the hundredth
> time, come back.

Though there was great hope that Allah would grant forgiveness, the Sufi had to seek it with total sincerity, and he knew that the grace of God would be better manifested if he cooperated; repentance could not be achieved by words alone but by preventing future occurrences of such deeds. He even had to make an effort to uproot the thought of these deeds. The supreme test for the seeker was to dispel all fictions, the world of carelessness (ghiflat), and initiate sincerity in action and purity in feeling.

The best example of such a case appears in Rumi's Mathnawi (Book V), which is known as tawba, the repentance of Nasuh. In this story, Rumi uses the analogy that just as milk flows from the teat never to return to the teat, so too he who repents from a sin should never return to the desire which caused his sin. However, before introducing the story, one should say that as tawba gradually takes root in the Sufi's heart, his loathing of sin will increase. The loathing is certainly proof that the seeker is succeeding in his tawba. His repentance has been accepted and the old lustful motives no longer exert any effect on him. In other words, the *tawba* has protected his character. If on the other hand, the seeker's heart is again directed toward a lustful sin, it definitely indicates that the seeker is still not steadfast in his conviction and repentance. In other words, when he has committed a lustful act, he has been under a strong urge which has blinded him to other alternatives. Now, if he truly seeks rebirth, he must be so committed to his repentance that nothing will dislodge him from this conviction. Finally, the lustful urge can only be broken by another love. The therapeutic significance is obvious. Recognition of the sin followed by repentance does not produce personality change. The spectrum of undesirable behaviours, including neuroticism, compulsiveness, impulsiveness, etc., must be replaced by a healthy dynamism initiated by the intention of *tawba* (repentance). The story of Nasuh in the *Mathnawi* provides a good example.

Nasuh was a man who earned a living by serving as a female masseur and attendant in a first class bath-house. As custom decreed that men could not work in the women's bath quarters, he therefore disguised his manliness, a contrived deceit, for although he managed to appear as a woman, his youthful lust was strong. He satisfied this lust by massaging and attending the princesses. Nasuh often repented but his carnal soul made him break his conviction. He once went to a great gnostic who served as a protector of people's secrets and asked him to pray for him. Though he said nothing, the holy man knew Nasuh's secret and said, 'May God help you in your repentance.' The prayer was answered by God in the following incident. One day when Nasuh was attending a princess, she lost one of her most valuable pearl earrings. The bath-house was thereafter closed, and the manager began a thorough search of the quarters and summoned every female attendant in order to search them. Stricken with fear, Nasuh's face paled, his lips turned blue and he began to tremble like a willow tree. He sought refuge in a private corner. The fear of being discovered was more frightening than the missing pearl earring. At any moment he felt he would die, because he knew that if his turn came to be searched, he would receive the cruellest punishment, more than any deceitful person could receive. As his anguish increased he prayed for mercy and lamented, 'Oh God, thou art the Lord Master in concealing man's sin. If you conceal my sin once more, I will sincerely repent every sinful act. If I break this conviction then hear no more prayers of this sinful creature.'

He sobbed as he lamented his fate while awaiting his turn to be searched. He heard the chief attendant exclaim, 'We have searched everyone now except Nasuh. Search Nasuh.'

Hearing his summons, Nasuh collapsed on the floor and fell into unconsciousness. In such a state he received divine mercy. Just as he lost consciousness he fully submitted to his true repentance, *tawba*. At almost the same moment that Nasuh collapsed, an attendant found the missing jewel. Now everyone's concern was directed to Nasuh to bring him to consciousness. He awakened to a new life: for while unconscious his former lustful self had departed from him, and he was born again to a new self. Nasuh declared,

> 'I died [a carnal self] once [and for all], and [then] I came back [to a spiritual life]. I tasted the bitterness of death and non-existence [Now I realize the value of life]. I have turned to God with the real repentance. I will not break the vow till my soul shall be parted from my body.' (Nicholson translation: *Mathnawi*, Book V).

His repentance and loyalty to his new conviction were so firm that he never responded to the princess's desire, though she repeatedly requested him to bathe and massage her. Each of these times Nasuh artfully managed to excuse himself. The importance of this excuse should be measured in terms of the fact that rejection of a princess's desire even now in a dictatorship is totally impossible. Nevertheless, Nasuh stood by his conviction and answered: 'Begone, begone! My hand is not in practice and your friend Nasuh has now fallen sick. Go seek some one else immediately and quickly, for by God's will my hands can no longer serve you.'

As Nasuh's loathing of his previous job increased, his *tawba* took root within his heart, and his loathing was certainly proof that he had succeeded in his *tawba*.

Wara *or* parhiz, *abstinence from wrong-doing (fear of God)*

Success in attaining *tawba* (repentance) largely depends on the sincerity of the seeker and his will to control the psychic situation so that he does not regress to become again the victim of earlier false values and desires relating to his life style. Thus, the seeker must pursue the next two stages which support his mental state and strengthen his *tawba*. The first of these twin stages is known as *wara or parhiz*, which literally means abstinence and avoidance of whatever the seeker believes is not godly. If one is uncertain of the outcome of his action he is better off to avoid it, or at least postpone such an act. Some authorities have translated *wara* as 'fear of the Lord', meaning that a seeker should avoid deeds which may be identified as producing human expectation or promises. In other words, if one fails to deliver the promise, it causes anger, displeasure, and above all, one loses credibility. Loss of credibility deprives a man of his mental support. In dealing with spiritual transcendance, the seeker must be ever careful, especially if he has deliberately chosen the path himself. He must avoid loss of credibility, he must abstain from anything which might cause the separation of himself and his lord: the purpose is to keep his mind positive in seeking his goal. Thus, he must adopt the step of *wara* and always be aware of his dissatisfaction. If in love he must guard his feelings so that he does not fall into a situation like that of Nasuh who adopted *tawba* numerous times and each time broke his vow until he almost faced death and only then achieved his *tawba* by the grace and prayer of the gnostic.

In fact, in the application of *wara*, the seeker is supposed to act as a watch-dog who is protecting his surroundings even when he appears to be slumbering. As a watch-dog he must train himself to watch over the heart and his own desires, chart the path of progress and avoid whatever might deter him in his pursuit of the path of self-transformation. It is essential to realize that 'whatever' refers here to every conceivable thing, idea, or deed, whether it is material possessions or human relations, including friends, relatives, or family, or matters concerning conventional faith. When one passes into the world of Sufis, through the bridge of intentional isolation, one must then destroy the bridge and look ahead with no regrets, because such a thought would indicate uncertainty and insincerity. To further strengthen the psychological state of the seeker so that he can benefit most from the stage of *wara*, the Sufis created the stage of *zuhd*, meaning complete detachment from one's previous world. We have already described this stage by using the analogy of the bridge, and in reality, this stage is a corollary to the stage of *wara*, which requires further explanation here. When the Sufis speak of detachment they do not mean merely physical detachment, but the *process* of detachment, whereas *wara* is the act of restraining the course of one's desire and observing one's inner world (one's stream of consciousness), *zuhd* means detachment from the root of the desire. The unity of desire, feeling, hand and heart must be achieved and confirmed by speech and supported by hearing or even touch. The diversity of senses should disappear so that one becomes all 'hearing', 'seeing', and all 'feeling' when observing a desire. The element of that desire should be dissected and uprooted so that one will have no desire. It is said that Bayazid Bastami, a master Sufi of the ninth century, enjoyed eating dates, but for the practice of *zuhd* he denied himself this pleasure for thirty years, until he no longer had any desire to eat one. In like manner, it is related that when a novice Japanese Zen disciple asked if he could have ice cream for a snack, the Zen master sent him out to buy ice cream for all. Then one of the disciples turned to the master and asked, 'The disciple desires ice cream, the master requires ice cream; then what is the difference?' To which the Zen master answered, 'If there were no ice cream tomorrow, the Zen master would not miss it, but the disciple would still have the desire.'

In terms of social conduct one must realize that elimination of certain behaviour means removal of hypocrisy. One eliminates the duality between saying one thing but doing another. The insincere acts of politicians, clergy, and false guides have no place here. Hafiz, the fourteenth-century Master Sufi and lyricist, exposed the hypocrisy of the clergy of his era. He wrote, 'The greatest social damage is done by those clergy who say "this" on the pulpit, but do "that" in private.' Sa'di, his predecessor, aptly remarked, 'No one can change morality by preaching.'

In other words, in the third stage one becomes *zahid*, the seeker of *zuhd*. However, one must always remind oneself that one's detachment is not from the external or phenomenal world, but from psychic determinism and from functional sources of desire. To further illustrate this stage, I must refer to the hypocrisy of those modern Hindus, Muslims or African students who come to the West for training and then forsake prayer as soon as they put on a tie. There are also those who make a point of praying in public in order to capitalize on popular sentiments. On a trans-Atlantic crossing, I once met a Hindu student who had spent five years in the United States. Finding him depressed, I tried to cheer him up. Finally he explained, 'I am depressed because for the last four years I have been eating meat, smoking, and acquiring worldly pleasures. Now that I am returning to India, I must live with my parents, who are even opposed to eating meat. How can I live with them and conceal my desires from them?'

On another occasion, I met a westernized Iranian youth who was ashamed of his grandmother putting on a veil in public. When I explained to him that the veil offered the old lady mental and physical security, he began to realize that his efforts could only create anxiety in his grandmother.

These examples of modern man's attachments are what the Sufis consider superficial. Through the stages of *zuhd*, the Sufis try to draw out the desire underlying the behaviour or even encourage the seeker to detach himself from the goal of detachment so that his feelings flow without reservation towards the one goal, Allah. By removing visible and invisible obstacles and psychic blocks, total liberation then occurs, and the seeker can relate to the essence and prepare himself for the next stage, poverty, that is, the realization that an empty heart is more important than having an empty hand. However, before discussing the next stage, it should be noted that many people in traditional Islamic society resigned from social reality (an outcome of centuries of calamities, particularly the twelfth to fifteenth centuries) and denounced the external world to become *zahid*. Though these men were pious and dealt with their own lives and harmed no one, they should not be confused with the Sufi seekers who adopted *zuhd* in order to detach themselves from various external and internal forces for gaining enlightenment and transcendental grace.

Faq'r (*poverty, or irreducible simplicity*)

Having progressed from the stages of *tawba* (repentance), *wara* (avoidance of wrong doing), and *zuhd* (detachment from all hindrances), the seeker now reaches the crux of the matter, that is, a heart and mind cleansed of everything, and certainty that the state of irreducible simplicity, total detachment, has occurred and will continue, such that it is a constant instead of a transitional happening. The inner condition of this state far exceeds the outer condition. Thus, a Sufi seeker may have material possessions and' riches provided he can stay detached from them. In fact, the emphasis on giving up physical attachments and possessions and forsaking social status, luxury, and titles is used as a training exercise, because to change a formed habit is more difficult than changing one's dwelling, profession, or spouse. However, to arrive at a mirror-like heart, a sensitive psyche, receptive organism and a state of total presence is not so easy; to remain in that state even harder. To understand the significance of this state requires a thorough understanding of its nature and insight into its gradual development and cultivation. Such an achievement is so great that Muhammad the Prophet attributed his revelations to it and considered such a psychic state his pride; on occasion he narrated: '*Al Faq'r e*

Fakhri' ('Poverty is my pride', where poverty refers to emptiness of the heart). Hafiz, the great Shirazi poet who got his messages in such a transcendental state, considered the state of poverty as the highest level of man's ascendance:

> *I am the slave of that courageous man,*
> *who can liberate himself from all*
> *worldly attachments that exist under the heavens.*

In a lecture on the re-examination of modern man, I have emphasized that political freedom, that is, liberty as based on human rights, is not enough. If man does not capitalize on this precious gift and proceed to liberate himself from whatever debases his true nature he will find that social freedom has turned to social lawlessness. In other words, freedom according to reason and social laws provides an opportunity for one to gradually discover its arbitrary status and free himself from it voluntarily. In another verse, Hafiz described the state of being of Assef, a vizier whom he admired, because with all his power and dignity, Assef possessed an inner state of total 'poverty':

> *I [Hafiz] humbly bow to the vizier*
> *who has the outward look of Assef*
> *and the inner spirit of a Sufi.*

However, if we are to thoroughly understand the nature of the state of 'poverty' (i.e. the state of *faq'r*), we must search the folklore of the Sufis, for folklore was often used then to combat men in powerful positions, to ridicule the very rich, and even to put aside man-made notions about God. Among many Sufi stories, the following story of 'nothingness' beautifully describes the stage of poverty and reveals the idea that irreducible simplicity, as a state of living, far surpasses the possession of wealth, rank, power and fame, even though each of these key states is rooted in historical reality.

According to the Sufi story, a great Oriental court once held a magnificent banquet where everyone was seated according to his rank while awaiting the appearance of the king. At that moment a plain, simply dressed man entered the hall and took a seat above everyone else. His boldness angered the Prime Minister, who demanded that he identify himself and acknowledge if he were a vizier. The stranger replied that he ranked above a vizier, and the astonished Prime Minister then asked if he were a prime minister. Again, the stranger replied that he was above that position. When asked if he were the king himself, he answered that he ranked above that too.

'Then you must be the Prophet', declared the Prime Minister; to which the man again asserted that he was above that position. Angrily, the Prime Minister shouted, 'Are you then God?' The man calmly replied again, 'I am above that too.' Contemptuously, the Prime Minister asserted, 'There is nothing above God.' In reply the man answered, 'Now you know my identity. That *nothing* is me.'

In other words, the Sufis sought to lose what they currently perceived as labels, knowledge, and concepts, and to become empty and attain the state of 'void', to attain a zero point so that they could become related to any state of being and achieve 'everythingness'. Just as the discovery of zero in mathematics made the system possible, so too in the art of rebirth the discovery of a state of 'nothingness' (the void or emptiness) makes final integration a possibility.

This story further teaches us that the process of identification with God is the means of avoiding all else except His image, and then when one has become Him, this becomes that and nothing remains; one becomes a true believer who has broken through the barrier of submission. The Master Sufi, Abu Yazid Bestami, along with al-Hallaj, is the best example. Yazid reportedly declared, 'For thirty years God was my mirror, now I am my own mirror.' What he meant was that through the stage of poverty he had totally liberated himself and had gradually filled up his psychic heart and total being with God's qualities to such an extent that he was He. Following is Abu Yazid's own description:[2]

> He laid the crown of munificence on my head, and opened unto me the door of the palace of Unity. When He perceived that my

attributes were annihilated in His attributes, He bestowed on me a name of His own presence and addressed me with His own Selfhood. Singleness became manifest; duality vanished.

He said, 'Our pleasure is that which is thy pleasure, and thy pleasure is that which is Our pleasure. Thy speech admits no defilement, and none takes thee to task on account of thy I-ness.'

Then He made me to taste the stab of jealousy, and revived me anew. I came forth pure from the furnace of testing. Then He spoke.

'Whose is the Kingdom?'

I said, 'Thine.'

He said, 'Whose is the Command?'

I said, 'Thine.'

He said, 'Whose is the Choice?'

I said, 'Thine.'

Since these words were the very same as He had heard at the beginning of the transaction, He desired to demonstrate to me that, had not His mercy preceded, creation would never have found repose, and that but for Love, Omnipotence would have wreaked destruction on all things. He gazed on me with the eye of Overwhelming through the medium of Allcompelling, and once more no trace of me was visible.

In my intoxication I flung myself into every valley. I melted my body in every crucible in the fire of jealousy. I galloped the steed of questing in the broad expanse of the wilderness; no better game I saw than utter indigence, nothing I discovered better than total incapacity. No lamp I saw brighter than silence, no speech I heard better than speechlessness. I became a dweller in the palace of silence; I clothed myself in the stomacher of fortitude, till matters reached their crux. He saw my outward and inward parts void of the law of fleshly nature. He opened a fissure of relief in my darkened breast, and gave me a tongue of divestiture and unity.

So now I have a tongue of everlasting grace, a heart of light divine, an eye of godly handiwork. By His succour I speak, with His power I grasp. Since through Him I live, I shall never die. Since I have reached this stage, my token is eternal, my expression everlasting; my tongue is the tongue of unity, my spirit is the spirit of divestiture. Not of myself I speak, that I should be mere narrator, neither through myself do I speak, that I should be mere remembrancer. He moves my tongue according as He wills, and in all this I am but an interpreter. In reality the speaker is He, not I.

Now, having magnified me, He spoke again.

'The creatures desire to see thee.'

I said, 'I desire not to see them. If Thou likest to bring me forth before the creatures, I will not oppose Thee. Array me in Thy Unicity, that when Thy creatures see me and gaze upon Thy handiwork, they will have seen the Artificer, and I shall not be there at all.'

This desire He granted me; and He laid the crown of munificence on my head, and caused me to surpass the station of my fleshly nature.

Then He said, 'Come before My creatures.'

I took one step out of the Presence. At the second step I fell headlong. I heard a cry.

'Bring back My beloved, for he cannot be without Me, neither knows he any path save to Me.'

As we mentioned in Chapter 4, al-Hallaj, in like manner but with greater courage, claimed that he was creative truth – in union with God. He further believed that when the veil of duality between creature and creator vanishes, the creative truth remains, and that is the real prayer.

In describing the function of this stage, Hafiz tells his audience that all thoughts of self must vanish from the psyche so that the empty cup of the soul can fill itself up with the beloved (God):

All ideas of Self have evaporated from my psyche, such that the horizon of my soul is surrounded by the ether of the Beloved.

Likewise, Rumi gives us an even more delicate analogy of this stage when he explains how the veins were emptied of blood and then filled again with the love of the Beloved:

Love came and I gave up my soul to the Beloved,
The Beloved now gives me life from His own life . . . .
Love came and like blood filled my veins and tissues,
Emptied me of myself and filled me with the Friend.
The friend has taken possession of every atom of my being.
The name is all that I have left now: all the rest is He.

So significant is the idea of poverty (al faq'r) in Sufi self-transformation that whatever other steps they took, even the hardship they bore – all their efforts were directed towards the realization of this stage and its continuation as a permanent state. It suffices to say that the Sufis believed that when the stage of poverty completes itself, God reveals Himself.

66

However, it was not only the image of the stage which was difficult, its process was even more difficult, and it exerted greater pressure on the seeker. Every detachment (physical, social, emotional, or mental) definitely produced a great anxiety and the seeker became *mutahayyr*, that is, bewildered. The pressure of this bewilderment was sometimes so intense that Sufis lost consciousness, just as in the previously mentioned case of Nasuh. When the Sufis re-entered the state of consciousness, they often became indifferent. In other words, their value orientation had been totally affected and they often ignored what the public believed in. On occasion the blame heaped upon them by the public was taken by the Master Sufi as a sign of their progress. During this period if the seeker went too far in seeking poverty, the master would send him to face ordinary life for two reasons, first to test the seeker, because public opinion would blame him for what he had achieved. Certain sincere Sufis accepted the blame with joy because they knew that their intentional isolation and effort had changed the structure of their psyche. The second reason for sending the seeker to face social life was that the master would feel that the seeker needed a fresh start; otherwise he might fall into an illusion. He therefore gave his disciple a respite before letting him proceed further in the process of purification.

This test often produced a redirection of motives, that is, the seeker became indifferent to choice. Everything seemed to have a genuine life of its own and appeared the same. Not only did 'choice' disappear, but hoped-for reward or fear of punishment likewise vanished. Thus, the Sufi prepared himself to cultivate tranquillity, and to perform actions which would strengthen his state of poverty and make him sensitive to receive the grace of God. However, caution was still required, for the process of the stage of poverty was so full of hardship and mental agony that it would have traumatized many Sufis if they had not received psychological support from the two subsequent stages – *sabr* (patience), and *tawakul* (trust in God).

Sabr provides a protection from insult and is the key to joy. Without *sabr* the experiences which make the stage of poverty possible would not have occurred and without *tawakul* (trust in God), the Sufi would not have dared to undertake that experience with courage. It is *sabr* which gave the Sufi endurance and perseverance. In fact, faith in action was tested by *sabr;* the greater the virtue of *sabr*, the stronger the faithful. *Sabr* was the shield which warded off the hidden afflictions of the path. The grace of God appeared with the exercise of patience, with steadfastness in action, and with perseverance in the process of acquiring poverty. Furthermore, *sabr* was the master's tool as well as that of the Sufi seeker. The master tested the seeker by examining the novice's capacity for patience, for the master knew that 'isolation' (the observation of one's own stream of consciousness) was a sorrowful activity which would only change to joy if, and only if, the Sufi exercised patience.

Patience alone would transform the sorrow of this separation into ultimate final peace of heart. The image of the beloved (Allah, all, the essence, etc.) would appear only within the mirror-like psyche; this would produce *gham* (grief of attainment). However, the psyche cannot be cleaned overnight: unlearning takes place gradually as the state of knowledge becomes no-knowledge; it is a long process of removing the cultural, historical and religious veils, and it is achieved through effort, but the effort itself often achieves little, and patience must become one's companion at this point, for the goal is a high mountain peak, the trail from the valley disappears in the forest, the slope is steep, and one needs great energy and patience to ascend. Hafiz, who recognized the hardship of the path, compared it to a dangerous voyage during a stormy night: how difficult it would be for those sleeping peacefully on shore to understand the condition of such a seafarer:

> In the midst of the dark night, in the midst of such a dangerous whirlpool, surrounded by frightening waves, how can our state be realized by the peaceful inhabitants of the quiet shore!

The effort of (*kushish* or *mujahada*) results in further progress only by patience, where patience makes the experience bearable and, if continued, produces signs and symbols of attaining poverty. *Tawakul* (self-surrender, trust in Allah) is the aim, and one's union with all is essential for every act. Thus every Sufi seeker begins his act 'in the name of Allah', that is, act for the sake of act.

The Sufi seeker could know the end in the mirror of the beginning only by trusting in God. Every courageous step brought him closer to total separation; detachment was full of danger and the Sufi gained courage from trust. Muhammad is supposed to have said: 'With trust in God tie the camel's knee and sleep in peace; don't worry about the danger.' *Tawakul* has always been a strong tenet of Islam and is implicit within the word Islam itself. Some Sufis even believe that *tawakul* was a natural development from patience and developed within the seeker gradually. In either case, *tawakul* made a great psychological contribution to the Sufi seeker. Though genuine effort is required from the Sufi, success is granted by the grace of God. Though medicine is applied by the physician, the cure is a gift from the almighty. Thus at every step in the Sufi's courageous process of emptying himself, the mental support came from Allah. *Tawakul* was therefore a means of strengthening one's separation from the present world and away from the demands of worldly mentality to attain relatedness to divine unity. As Sufis were totally devoted to divine unity, they began every action by chanting the name of Allah. On one occasion a disciple asked Abu Yazid what his state of being was; the master wrote on a piece of paper: 'In the name of Allah, the most kind and merciful', and added that it was his own state. Second, trust in God is the means of getting away from ego and surrendering one's self. In this respect, *tawakul* became self-surrender and encompassed all previous stages. It was a process of becoming God-like. The Sufi sought to lose his phenomenal self, dispose of what the environment had cultivated in him, and utilize the image of God as motivation for attraction (*jazba*) and divine unity.

Following this stage, the Sufi gradually arrived at *reza*, the point where he felt he was being accepted, and 'joyous satisfaction' overcame him. This stage was sometimes considered as a state (mental *hal*). However, it served as the line between effortful stages and the states of being, which we will soon discuss. In any case, the condition of the Sufi was total accept- ance of whatever gift he received. Furthermore, he was satisfied with it. This *reza* was thus a state of mutual satisfaction in the trinity of the Sufi, the guide, and God. It was due to this quality that the experience appeared to some as an effortless illumination. It was a mystical state which happened without acquisition. In every effortless illumination the Sufi released himself of self-consciousness. Its repetition brought his true self closer to cosmic self. In other words, it was the state of total contentment which increased the seeker's love of his journey. The stage of *reza* was further characterized by the elimination of all demands and requests; the seeker was now cut off from the past, he had no wishes for the future, and patiently waited for the creative presence. Through his efforts in passing through the previous six stages, he had now attained 'emptiness', which functioned as a sharp sword, cutting off the past from the future. In this condition, the seeker patiently waited so that the inner experience of satisfaction could make his state a constant one. He could then join the group known as *ahl-e-reza*, those who were content with what they were and satisfied with God and with living. In fact, all that *reza* meant was that the Sufi's inner mind was in harmony with the creative wheel of the universe, and he, the Sufi, lived, acted, and died for God's sake, for the act itself, and unconditionally.

Psychic states: an analysis of the process of inner change

After the long conscious effort (*kushesh* or *riaza*), the seeker achieves poverty and continuous tranquility through 'patience' and 'trust' in the world. The last stage, *reza*, total satisfaction, is definitely a two-sided coin. One side is the result of the previous stages which give conscious satisfaction of one's self, while on the more significant side is the mark of total psychic content- ment without consciousness. However, the attainment of this final state requires the experiencing of gradual illumination, culminating in divine unity.

Whereas progress in the outer self, in the purification of achieved self, was attained through *kushesh* (conscious effort), progress in the inner self came through *keshesh-jazba* (divine attraction). In fact, the nature of man, after the attainment of the stage of poverty, undergoes a reversal; he actively sharpens his receptive antenna in order to receive the current of life. Perhaps such a person becomes an instrument of the living stream of communication, hidden within the universe. As the intensity of *kedesh-jazba* (divine attraction) increases, the individual passes from one state to another.

There are eight to ten states, and between states there are innumerable *ahwal* (the plural of *hal*), that is, changing psychic conditions. To describe such a subtle change is difficult. If one goes through the experience of this inner change, one gradually becomes a part of those inner insights, and basically that is attaining illumination. However, certain analogies have been used. One classic Sufi analogy is that the psyche is a total darkroom and dominated by nothing except intense darkness. Now with a particular experience of union, a candle light appears in the dark chamber of the psyche. A second experience brings a second candle light, and so on, until all the chambers are illuminated, and more intense experiences illuminate the psyche in such a high intensity that nothing remains but light. Once at the University of Hawaii, I was asked by a sceptical member of the audience, 'What shall we do when we reach such a final state?' I responded spontaneously to the level of his understanding:

'A few hours ago I arrived in Honolulu by jet from Tokyo, and if you had not met me, I would not have known how to get to the hotel, and from there to the University. Now if you don't accompany me back to the hotel, I will not be able to find my way to the city very easily; however, if I stay in Hawaii a few weeks, I will become aware of roads, signs, symbols and even the sea around the island. So too, the gradual development of the inner psyche is a similar process but its exploration is invisible, and it often takes place like a strong current under the surface of the sea and the experience of it requires changing conditions. The change is gradual and depends upon the ascendence of the psyche in various states.'

Although the inquirer seemed satisfied and did not pursue the matter, I did not think he was a sincere person who would follow the slow and arduous path of psyche illumination. However, if a courageous man pursues the path, he will experience the following states, known as *maqamat*:

1 *muraqaba*, observation of one's psyche
2 *qurb*, the experience of approaching one's goal (union)
3 *showq*, intense longing for divine unity
4 *mehr*, unconditional love for all
5 *omid*, the hope for getting nearer
6 *uns*, intimacy
7 *mushahida*, contemplation on the unitary experience
8 *itmianan*, state of securing the self
9 *yaqin*, certainty.

Muraqaba (*observation of the psychic stream*)

Being now in the sensitive stage of poverty, the seeker spends his total being in stabilizing that state. He must not think, feel, or do anything which is not God-like. A state is definitely more stable than a *hal*, for a *hal* is comparable to a train in motion, whereas a state is akin to stations which one passes until his train finally reaches its ultimate destination. Numerous *ahwal* exist between the stages. Thus *muraqaba* is like the first station in the path of inner psyche. The seeker can rest here and strengthen himself by experiencing the presence of God at all times. Jurjani, an authority on classical Sufism, succinctly states that the seeker in the state of *muraqaba* should remind himself that 'he is either in the *hal* of observing God in action or in the *hal* where God observes him.' When one is in such a state there will be no opportunity for feeling, thinking, or doing wrong. Furthermore, by observing creation through the names of Allah, one gradually internalizes the creative process and becomes intensified concentration. It is believed that Shibli, a well-known Baghdad Sufi master of the ninth century, once visited Nuri, a contemporary master Sufi. It happened that Nuri was in the state of *muraqaba* and his intense concentration surprised Shibli; in fact the visitor could not even detect his breathing. When Nuri came out of this state, that is, when he became aware of Shibli (who had been waiting a long time), Shibi asked him 'From which master did you learn this great depth of *muraqaba*?' Nuri responded simply, 'From a cat watching a mousehole. But the cat could still concentrate better than I.'

The story is also reminiscent of Socrates, who during the defence of Athens is supposed to have occasionally put himself into a state of concentration from sunset to sunrise. Likewise, history reveals that during the battle of Chalderan between the Persian Shah Ismail Safavi (sixteenth century) and the Ottoman Turks, Shah Ismail had no guns though his enemy did. It is said that just before the battle Shah Ismail leaned against a tree and fell into deep concentration over his predicament. Though his attendant brought him his water pipe three times, he failed to get his master's attention so deep was his concentration. Finally on the fourth time, the attendant remarked, 'Sir, this is the fourth time I have prepared your pipe', thereby disrupting Ismail's concentration. The king then came out of his state and replied, 'It doesn't matter now; I have just killed the gunner'. According to history, on the following day Shah Ismail with great heroic effort passed through the attacking Turkish army, reached the gunner, and ran his sword through him, just as he had envisioned.

In order that one may achieve such a level of *muraqaba*, it is essential to make certain that one's motives for action are not self-indulgent, the desire for worldly goods merely for the sake of possession, fame or self-conceit. One must throw aside all social and intellectual veils and polish the mirror of the psyche so that the state of *muraqaba* overpowers the whole being. In fact, Sufism is nothing more than polishing the mirror of the psyche so that it fully reflects the essence of the universe. In other words, the Sufis believe that through this experience of socialization, moralization, and intellectualization, the creative sensitivity of man decreases, if not diminishes. In order for man to recapture his intuitive antenna and thus penetrate the surface, he must unveil his true receptive condition.

The contrast between this mirror-like ability of the psyche and the ordinary intellectual approach is beautifully described in the story of a contest between Chinese and Greek artists which was told in Chapter 3.

The state of qurb (nearness to God, the love object)

Just as the actualization of *faq'r* (poverty) was a preparation for the state of *muraqaba*, which in turn prepared the seeker for the state of *qurb*, so too did *qurb* bring the individual nearer to fulfilment, God, and passage to unity – the key to the transformation of the soul. Early Sufis relied upon invocations, and the content of their *zikr* (invocation) was drawn from the Qur'an. There were those who chanted only the names of Allah, which symbolically encompassed the whole universe. Some selected single names such as *Alim* (all-knowing), *Basir* (all-noticing), *Sa'mia* (all-hearing), *al-rahim* (the most benevolent), *al-rahman* (the kindest), and the like. There were also those who borrowed phrases from the Qur'an, such as *la ilaha ill'Allah* (There is no God but Allah), or merely *Hu* (He), or sometimes they repeated a whole verse from the Holy Book, such as *Kull e Shayin Hallik alla vajhahu* (All things pass away except His face), and contemplated nothing else until the seekers' souls were submerged in the sea of the Holy Book. By employing the methods of *muraqaba* (concentration on the meaning of their invocation) and *mushahida* (contemplation of the essence), these seekers tried to purify themselves. However, the Master Sufis differentiated between the invocation of God's name by repetition (*tekrar*) and the invocation founded on the search for meaning (*tahqiq*). Authorities such as al-Ghazzali and Najmudin Razi recognized the value of repetition, but also emphasized the importance of *zikr* for meaning. Thus, while the seeker should start the *zikr* verbally, he must gradually concentrate his mind on it and search for the meaning. For instance, the Sufi seeker must contemplate on such a *zikr* as 'There is no God but God', and try to discover the fact that the essence of everything is life, and life is that indefinable, mysterious, and natural existence we call God. Having accepted this phrase mentally, he should then turn to the heart and remember the verse from the Qur'an where God says that heaven and earth may not remember Him, but the heart of man can do so. Invocation must penetrate the heart so that it becomes effective. It is through this medium that identification with God takes place. Through the stages, Sufis believed that man can empty himself of everything, just as Jesus did, and then fill himself with God. The gateway to Heaven is man's heart. In *Final Integration in the Adult Personality* when I examined the failure and achievement of modern Western psychology, I stated that all systems of psychology teach us one Sufi reality, that is, 'Ideas which are not rooted in emotion can hardly be materialized.' The importance of practising invocation for unification and insight, for purifying the soul and finding the true path by the process of *qurb* is illustrated in the following story of the moth and the candle.

It is said that on a dark night a group of moths, puzzled by the light of a candle, hovered around the lighted chamber. The leader of the group wanted to know the essence of light and after informing the group of his desire, he sent a scout to find out the nature of the light. The scouting moth flew to the window and finally approached the candle light and repeatedly circled around it. He circled innumerable times, and when he returned to the group he described the light as brilliant. The leader sent the second scout and asked him to discover the nature of light; he could see that it was brilliant from his position, even though far removed from it. The second scout reached the light, examined it, and tried to get as close as possible; he felt the heat and when he returned he described it was warm and having a burning quality. The leader was not satisfied by the scout's knowledge. He then flew toward the candle and penetrated it. He was consumed in the light and thereby showed the rest that it was only by being consumed that they would be able to know the true nature of things. Likewise, the Sufi *zikr* took on added dimensions for the Sufis. The repetition of holy names and certain spiritual phrases helped the seeker get closer to his objectives, but contemplation was still more desirable and further contemplation on the meaning of the names of God was the most desirable.

On achieving this goal, the seeker was then supposed to perform the *zikr* in a prescribed manner. After his intention, the seeker had to clean himself physically by taking a bath, then don a clean robe and receive guidance from the master. He then went to his *zavia* (quarters), sat cross-legged facing *qabla* (Mecca), put his hands on his thighs and began his *zikr* verbally, gradually concentrating on the meaning and intensifying his concentration until his heart was totally absorbed by it. He would then begin to feel that his heart was performing the *zikr*. At this time he would stop repeating it verbally and move along with feeling. If his feelings lost intensity he would repeat the *zikr* until he was again immersed in it. Sometimes a master organized a group *zikr* for greater effectiveness, and as I shall indicate, the group *zikr* was often used at the beginning of the *sa'ma* (music with spiritual circular dancing).

By means of *zikr*, *qurb* takes place and the seeker feels closer and closer to the essence of the reality of beings. He enters the climax of his own being, that is, he is prepared by *qurb* to get to the state of *uns* (intimacy with God) and His representation.

The state of uns (*the discovery of the unity of life and diversity of forms*)

When the seeker achieved *qurb* by means of *muraqaba* and *mushahida* he got closer to God's image; he wished to remain in that association and become intimate. Thus the process was called *uns* (literally 'intimacy'). To realize the significance of intimacy, one can make it perceivable by remembering environmental experiences. In my own experience, I once visited my home town, Shiraz, after an absence of sixteen years. As a schoolboy I had had the early morning custom of walking down neighbourhood streets and alleys to school. So familiar were the cobble stones to me, even after sixteen years, that my feet seemed aware of individual stones, some of which I instinctively avoided and others which I trod on lightly. Their colours, shapes and combinations were all meaningful. In an analagous way, the Sufi seeker by means of invocations would cultivate God-like qualities within himself in the hope of becoming intimate with them. For instance, one may associate the everlasting essence of life and love with God. Then believing that everything is from Him and to Him we will return, the seeker can easily discover life in the sturdy little ant, in the busy bees, in plants, animals, and in a hidden way in all creatures. He may perceive that the very life essence has changed from inorganic to organic, the organic substance to living animals, to man; he then perceives a new form of life beyond this form.

This is the circle of being, going from non-human existence to trans-human existence. In other words, intimacy with God's manifestation (nature) makes the seeker's life meaningful. In fact, he may suddenly discover that life is within him, and in terms of life God is closer to him than his jugular vein. Thus the seeker passes through a 'Copernicus' type experience. But this time instead of seeking his greatest object of desire, God, outside of himself, he will discover God within himself. With this experience, he recognizes that ascendance of man to God becomes descendance of God to man. The seeker then experiences a unity in diversity of form and longs for greater intimacy. This longing is the next state, and it is known as *shugh* (longing). The increase of *shugh* and further separation from the orbit of intimacy is called *firaq*, genuine separation. Separation may appear in different degrees, but according to Sufism the most intense separation of man from God's image occurred when man became aware of himself and discovered the distance between himself and nature. Ever since man was cast from Paradise (his unconscious state in nature) he has longed for a new union. This intense separation at its fullest was experienced by Rumi, and its feelings beautifully conveyed at the beginning of *Mathnawi*:

> *Listen to the reed how it tells a tale, complaining of*
> * separation —*
> *Saying, 'Ever since I was parted from the reed-bed my*
> *Lament hath caused man and woman to moan.*
> *I want a bosom torn by severance, that I may unfold (to such*
> * a one) the pain of love-desire.*
> *Every one who is left far from his source wishes back the time*
> * when he was united with it.*
> *In every company I uttered my wailful notes, I consorted with*
> * the unhappy and with them that rejoice.*
> *Every one became my friend from his own opinion, none*
> * sought out my secrets from within me.'*
>
> (*Book I, Nicholson translation*)

Furthermore, the experience of intimacy gives the seeker security and makes *firaq* (original separation) meaningful. Often the seeker longs for the intimacy which is a remedy to his *firaq*. To recapture the intimacy and make it a constant, the seeker changes the longing leading to increased 'love' for the beloved. In its purest form that state of love is identification of 'I' with 'thou', where 'thou' can be Allah — all that which exists, or in the words of Sa'di, the thirteenth-century Shirazi: 'I am in love with whatever I find, as everything I find is a manifestation of Him'. Or 'thou' can be a specific manifestation of Him just as the relationship the nightingale expresses for the rose, or that of a moth for candle light. Love is the result of 'I-thou' union, and according to such great Sufi masters as Rumi, the whole universe came into being through this process. It is here that the Sufis make the greatest contribution to the history of evolution. Unlike Darwin's ideal of survival of the fittest, the Sufi doctrine gives us 'survival through love'. In fact, according to Rumi, ordinary men and women erroneously think that 'lover and beloved' make 'love', whereas the Sufi believes that lover and beloved are born from 'love'. Love is the only mechanism of evolution. It appears as attraction between inorganic and plant life, as a strong feeling between human beings, and as consummation of man within God in the process of inner evolution. Rumi's poem expresses this basic idea:

The dame says to [chickpea]: Formerly I like thee, was a
    part of the earth
After I had drunk a [cup of] fiery self-mortification,
    then I became an acceptable and worthy one.
For a long while I boiled in [the word of] time; for
    another long while, in the pot of the body.
By reason of these two boilings I became [a source of]
    strength to the senses: I became [animal] spirit:
    then I became thy teacher.
[Whilst I was] in the inanimate state I used to say [to myself]:
Thou art running [to and fro in agitation] to the end that
    thou mayst become [endured with] knowledge and spiritual
    qualities.
Since I have become [anima] spirit, now [let me]
    boil once more and pass beyond animality.

                              (*Nicholson translation*, Mathnawi)

In another place, Rumi is even more expressive in believing
that the universe and its evolution arises from the process of
'love'. In fact, 'love' becomes the only vehicle of transformation:[3]

Through love thorns become roses, and
Through love vinegar becomes sweet wine
Through love the stake becomes a thorn
Through love the reverse of fortune seems good fortune,
Through love a prison seems a rose bower,
Through love a grate full of ashes seems a garden
Through love a burning fire is a pleasing light.
Through love the Devil becomes a Houri.
Through love the hard stone becomes soft as butter.
Through love grief is a joy.
Through love ghouls turn into angels.
Through love stings are as honey,
Through love lions are harmless as mice,
Through love sickness is as health
Through love wrath is as mercy.

Likewise the Sufi seeker penetrated every manifestation of nature. In fact, through love of beautiful forms, he tried to understand the essence of things. The Sufi theory of epistemology (if they at all believed in theorizing) was based on the process of love. Some Sufi masters, like Awhad al-Din Kirmani, even believed that it is impossible to penetrate the inner meaning of objects without first falling in love with their forms. He further believed that external expression is the key to understanding the inner world. From the dew drops on the jar one knows that water is in the jar; so too does the symbolic form guide us toward formless beauty. It is the exercise of loving beautiful form which strengthens the heart of the Sufi and his state of *uns*. From their observation of Nature and heavenly bodies, Sufi seekers gradually replaced the customary six directions (up and down, north and south, east and west) by one circular motion. Thus, long before the practical discovery of gravitational laws, the Sufis knew that the true nature of life and man was to be found in spherical motion; and they believed that revelation and other mystical truths would appear to them by spherical motion. Perhaps this intuitive discovery of the significance of spherical motion and gravitation led some of the great Sufis to break away from their formalistic prayer, and they adopted music and dance as a means of transcendence of the soul. Music was a far more superior language to their ears than words. In fact, the music of nature such as bird song and the rustling of the breezes, wind, and water elevated their state of being. Moreover, all forms of Persian poetry were adapted to a variety of chants and songs. Dance movements also served to convey free bodily and spiritual expressions. Almost all great Sufis discovered these two mechanisms of music and dance. The biographer of Abu Said (the predecessor of Rumi) records how the master Sufi performed ecstatic dances with some of his intimate disciples and so engrossed were they that they did not heed the Muezzin's call for mid-day prayers. When the Imam (prayer leader) approached him and sought to remind him, Abu-Said answered: 'We are in prayer'. Al-Ghazzali once wrote that just as greenery and external beauty harmonize our eyesight so too music harmonizes our inner world.

But no Sufi used music and dance as a systematic means for perfecting the soul and strengthening the state of love as did Mowlana Jalalalddin Rumi. To him the flute made out of a reed was a symbol of man's separation from his reed-bed, his origin. For Rumi music was the food of love and a means of harmonizing relatedness, which penetrated the form and related the Sufi to his inner-world. Rumi had further discovered that spherical motion was the one motion which could release the Sufi's energy and unify his various senses so that he might receive messages and be inspired. In fact, Rumi received such an inspiration from rotation, for he practically composed all of the *Mathnawi* while he was rotating around a column of his *khaneqa* and his scribe (himself a master) wrote down his verses. In my opinion, circular motion provides a basic means for moving man from a self-conscious state to a unitary insightful state where his soul can communicate to his beloved. Although Western 'intellectuals' in the past had no basis for comprehending such phenomena, they have now a better basis for understanding it because of their growing self-emancipation. A vivid description for the Sufi dances and music leading up to *zikr* was provided by Lane, the Egyptologist, who visited Egypt in the early nineteenth century. The following passage shows his keen observations, though he gives no interpretation:[4]

> Most of the durweeshes [*sic*] were Egyptians, but there were among them many Turks and Persians. I had not waited many minutes before they began their exercises. . . . Forty of them, with extended arms and joined hands had formed a large ring. . . . The durweeshes who formed the large ring (which enclosed four of the marble columns of the portico) now commenced their *zikr* exclaiming over and over again, 'Allah' and at each exclamation, bowing the head and body and taking a step to the right; so that the whole ring moved rapidly around. As soon as they commenced this exercise, another durweesh, a Turk, of the order of Mowlawees [refers to Rumi's order] in the middle of a circle, began to whirl; using both his feet to effect his motion and extending his arms: the motion increased in velocity until his dress spread out like an umbrella. He continued whirling thus for about ten minutes, after which he bowed to his superior, who stood within the great ring; and

then without showing any signs of fatigue or giddiness, joined the durweeshes in the great ring; who had now begun to ejaculate the name of God with great vehemence, and to jump to the right, instead of stepping. After whirling, six other durweeshes, within the great ring, formed another ring; but a very small one; each one placing his arms upon the shoulders of those next him; and thus disposed, they performed a revolution similar to that of the larger ring, except in being much more rapid; repeating, also, the same exclamation of 'Allah'; but with a rapidity proportionately greater. This motion they maintained for about the same length of time that the whirling of the single durweesh before had occupied; after which the whole party sat down to rest. They rose again after the lapse of about a quarter of an hour, and performed the same exercise a second time.

These circular dances reveal the Sufis' process of identification with spherical and heavenly order, the creation of total relaxation without 'bio-feedback' and finally their spiritual transcendence. However, music and dance as performed in the *sa'ma* followed strict rules and had to be done under the direction of a proper guide. Many reports have been written about master Sufis who were the musicians during the dances and whose disciples performed the dances. They played melodies according to the modes (*ahwal*) of the seekers and directed their inner change. The dance mechanism was used after meditation and according to prescribed rules for *zikr*, which I referred to previously. The steps of *muraqaba* and *mushahida* were utilized to enrich the Sufi state; then in a proper moment of readiness the disciple began a proper *zikr* until his inner frame of mind compelled him to use the dance for further illumination. Even though the above description by Lane is a vivid one, it emphasizes the colourfulness of the drama rather than viewing it as a natural occurrence, which I myself have seen in Kurdistan and elsewhere in Iran. Furthermore, the trio of events (music, dance and the singing of Persian lyrics) was masterfully used by the guide to transcend the state of the Sufi seekers. In the state of love and search for further *uns* the lyrics were intended as a gradual effort ultimately to bring about union, joy, and total cultivation of a positive attitude. Undoubtedly, there were orthodox religious leaders who could not accept this form of prayer, just as orthodox clergy today objects to new modes of prayer. Then as now there were immature individuals, including some of our youth today, whose neurotic energy finds an outlet in these kinds of dances. While such sessions may definitely calm the outward presence of such individuals, they contribute little to their inner growth as Sufis. On a recent visit to Arizona, I encountered such an 'orphan Sufi' group. Every Thursday night they came together, often without ordinary cleanliness, to dance wildly in the moonlight to loud music until exhausted. When I became acquainted with them I learned to my disappointment that their only attraction to Sufism arose from their rejection of their own society.

This phenomenon is not new. Sa'di in his travels in the thirteenth century keenly observed similar groups who did not understand or who misinterpreted the true ways of Sufism. To paraphrase some of his wisdom, Sa'di believed that one must not even speak of sa'ma before knowing who the believer was. If the listener was a frivolous and flippant individual, sa'ma would strengthen his state of being, and he would become more devilish. Then Sa'di proceeds to give a beautiful simile: 'flowers dance and are moved by the morning breeze, whereas the hard trunk of a tree needs an axe', or in other words, a gentle soul can be moved by sweet music, but a cold heart cannot be awakened by the beat of a drum.

On another occasion, Sa'di, in defence of sa'ma, says:

> Do not blame the Sufi in sa'ma,
> If he waves his hands and feet, the reason is that
>   he is drowning (in the sea of existence); and
> The dance opens in the soul a door to divine influences.
> Sufi's hands are spread wide to all created things and his
>   dance is genuine when it arises from a remembrance of
>   the Beloved (God).
> Then each moving sleeve has a soul in it.
> If you set out bravely to swim, you can best move arms and legs
>   when divested of clothing.
> Strip off the robes of earthly honour and hypocrisy,
> A drowning man is hampered by his clothes.

During my own life these last few verses from Sa'di greatly influenced my maternal grandfather, Al Sayyd Hirza, for both he and his father were advocates of Sufi saints. My grandfather thus summarizes the essence of Sufism in a dance which he performed with great joy when I was a child. I recall that when I was nine and in the fourth grade I spent the entire summer with my grandfather, who was then over sixty years old and active in cultivating grapes and honey bees. I vividly remember hiking with him hand in hand, climbing the mountain slopes that surrounded the summer resort of Ardekan near Shiraz. During these climbs, he proudly showed me the grapevines which he had tenderly cared for and planted among the rocky mountain slopes. Sometimes when we sat down to rest he removed the stones that he had carefully arranged around them to protect them from frost in the spring time. He performed his work with loving care. Often late at night when we were sitting on the roof of his house under the moonlight, I would ask him questions which puzzled me concerning the stories my mother had told me. When I asked him to explain how his father had been able to walk up the side of a wall, he would simply say, 'With Allah's grace an impossible task becomes simple.' Then he would use the analogy that if moonlight from miles away can pull the water of the sea upward, then perhaps there are certain bodies (including man) which are so light and pure that they can be easily lifted up in the air. He would then relate the case of the Prophet, who is believed to have ascended towards Heaven on certain occasions and the fact that the Prophet had also been able to put his finger-tips under his arms and then bring them forth, glowing in the dark. My grandfather also mentioned 'Attar, the Master Sufi of the twelfth century, and related how he had visited his shrine in Nishapur and described how the whole area of his dome had given him an inexplicable feeling of radiance. Then he would bring the conversation to an end by saying, 'My dear Reza, I am sure one of these days we will have more time to discuss these matters.' With these words and a hug I was sent to bed.

However, it was not until the summer of 1941 when I was

fourteen years old that I actually saw wonders performed around him. It was at this time when political prisoners, including tribal chieftains, were being released from prison; they were returning to Fars to reorganize their tribes and re-capture their property that Reza Shah had confiscated. My parents had left Shiraz before school was out. By the time I finished my final examinations, no public bus or other trans-portation dared to pass through that thirty- to forty-mile stretch because of bandits. Being anxious to join my family, particularly my grandfather, I finally located an army truck, whose driver told my cousin and me that we could ride on the load with the mail carrier. The truck, accompanied by an armoured tank, left Shiraz and proceeded cautiously along the route until we got to within one mile of the environs of Ardekan. Suddenly I saw the whole mountainside dotted with tribal riflemen, who began to shoot at us. The mail carrier received a shot in the leg just as my cousin, Agha Hassan, and I jumped down into the river which flows out of Ardekan. Fortunately, we were hidden from sight by the truck, and we quickly grabbed hold of the bushes on the river bank. Walking in water up to our chests, we moved out of rifle range and ran into Ardekan to take the news to the army post there. Then we hurried to my grandfather's home. Having spotted us from the roof of his house, he rushed down and embraced me, kissing me several times. Then in a prayer-like trance, which I had never wit-nessed before, he went into a circular movement and stepping out of the house he offered his green silken shawl to one passer-by, his beautiful robe to another. We were so exhausted that we could not even comprehend the scene, and we suddenly began to cry. Grandfather embraced us both, like two babies. When my parents appeared, grandpa turned to them and said, 'You must immediately sacrifice a lamb because today is a second birthday for Reza and Hassan.' Then he added, 'What I had hoped not to happen is approaching.' Then he proceeded to tell my parents that within the next three weeks a Mongul-type attack would take place in Ardekan. From early dawn he had been worried about this vision. Then he described his vision, which was almost identical to what we had gone through, except that he also foresaw the approaching tragedy. In fact, in twenty days time, the Boi-Rahmadis tribe (perhaps descendents of the Monguls who had at some time in the past penetrated the Fars mountains), attacked Ardekan. For twenty-four hours they took away whatever they found, rounded up the livestock, and loaded the animals with their stolen goods and then departed. I remember that during that terrifying night they entered our home seventeen times; they took away even the prayer rug on which my grandfather was reciting the Qur'an. They emptied the cooking pot and took the pot. All in all, it was a sad night: in every household some-one was weeping, especially in those homes where someone had tried to resist. Being in the household of a religious leader of the community, a descendant of Muhammad, the Prophet, we were safe, but every moment was filled with dread until the tribal chief rode out of Ardekan.

It was after this calamity that my grandfather began visiting and consoling every family. To bring out their genuine spirits again, he set up nightly sessions in order to spread the vision of sharing, as well as to convey the sublime Sufi idea that physical poverty is easily overcome if we are not shaken by spiritual poverty. Even more amazing was that he communicated the idea that we must eventually give up whatever we have; we must not be governed by sad events such as plunder, which we cannot understand, and we must come out of ourselves and reach for the 'other'. It was in these nightly sessions that I saw grandfather, not only chanting verses from various poets but performing a special dance, which the others joined in with him.

Grandfather considered this dance an expression of total humanity and an indication of human love for one's fellow men, as well as a means to illumination, and an experience of *An*, that is, the creative moment. His grace and stance were beyond the ability of any sixty-year-old man. The expression in his eyes was vivid and conveyed a sense of being totally at ease, relaxed, and utterly joyous. Grandfather would then gracefully take a step while bringing the palms of his hands toward his chest and reciting verses about 'phenomenal self'. Then he would pause before performing the second movement. At the right moment he began the second movement by reciting a poem or a verse to suggest that we leave, drop out the 'self', which is occupying us. Then he would bend gracefully while bringing the palms of his hands up in the air and dropping them toward the earth. This movement was followed by still more chanting about the essence of God while he raised his hands toward the heavens at the same time as he stood in prayer. Then he would take the fourth movement, chanting, 'We don't know, we don't know', and move the back of his hand over his shoulder giving a 'nay' sign. Then with a shining face and graceful manner he moved his right hand toward one of his intimate fellow Sufis and chanted 'You, you, you are all in all. Oh you, you are all in all'. Then he moved gracefully toward the left repeating the last motion toward another fellow Sufi, while chanting, 'You, you, you are all in all'. In turn, each of the fellows followed him, and a great spirit of fellowship, a spirit of unity and togetherness emanated from one to another.

While this was going on, my mother explained each of the movements and said simply, 'Your grandfather is trying to say that we must not be selfish; we must not question the essence of God but cultivate his attributes within us, and we must know that the greatest joy comes from our love for the "other".'

It was only years later when I wrote a paper on Sa'di, and still decades after grandfather's dance, while writing *Rumi the Persian, the Sufi*, that I really understood what my grandfather had wanted to convey to the leaders of Ardekan, both as individuals and as a group to rebuild the community.

State of unity

Now we come to the ultimate question: what were all these conscious and unconscious efforts for? They were definitely directed toward expanding consciousness from its limited social structure to cosmic designs. It served to recreate our unitary existence with the world. By the practice of love one could identify with the beloved, just as by gradual identification an apprentice becomes a master. However, as long as the image of the master remains within the apprentice a new soul has not been born; as long as the image of the father is within the child, maturity has not taken place; and as long as the image of God governs the Sufi, total identification with the cosmos (with God) has not been attained. The unity experience is gradual and is often achieved only by rare individuals who become so intimate with the cosmos that they dare to use 'I' and 'God' interchangeably. We have already spoken of al-Hallaj, who boldly revealed the secret and like Christ was crucified; but a better expression of this achievement was Abu-Yazid al-Bestami, whom we introduced earlier. However, it would be worthwhile to re-emphasize his process of the unity of experience. This experience of Bestami is beautifully described by 'Attar in the following words in his *Tadhkirat al-Auliya* (translation by Arberry):[5]

> I gazed upon God with the eye of curiosity after that He had advanced me to the degree of independence from all creatures, and illuminated me with His light, revealing to me the wonders of His secrets and manifesting to me the grandeur of His He-ness.
>
> Then from God I gazed upon myself, and considered well the secrets and attributes of my self. My light was darkness beside the light of God; my grandeur shrank to very meanness beside God's grandeur; my glory beside God's glory became but vainglory. There all was purity, here all was foulness.
>
> When I looked again, I saw my being by God's light. I realized that my glory was of His grandeur and glory. Whatsoever I did, I was able to do through His omnipotence. Whatever the eye of my physical body perceived, it perceived through Him. I gazed with the eye of justice and reality; all my worship proceeded from God, not from me, and I had supposed that it was I who worshipped Him.
>
> I said, 'Lord God, what is this?'
>
> He said, 'All that I am, and none other than I.'
>
> Then He stitched up my eye, not to be the means of seeing and so that I might not see, and He instructed the gaze of my eye to the root of the matter, the He-ness of Himself. He annihilated me from my own being, and made me to be everlasting through His own everlastingness ,and He glorified me. He disclosed to me His own Selfhood, unjostled by my own existence. So God,

the one Truth, increased in my reality. Through God I gazed on God, and I beheld God in reality.

There I dwelt a while, and found repose. I stopped up the ear of striving; I withdrew the tongue of yearning into the throat of disappointment. I abandoned acquired knowledge, and removed the interference of the soul that bids to evil. I remained still for a space, without any instrument, and with the hand of God's grace I swept superfluities from the pathway of root principles.

God had compassion on me. He granted me eternal knowledge, and put into my throat a tongue of His goodness. He created for me an eye out of His light, and I saw all creatures through God. With the tongue of His goodness I communed with God, and from the knowledge of God I acquired a knowledge, and by His light I gazed on Him.

He said, 'O thou all without all with all, without instrument with instrument!'

I said, 'Lord God, let me not be deluded by this. Let me not become self-satisfied with my own being, not to yearn for Thee. Better it is that Thou shouldst be mine without me, than that I should be my own without Thee. Better it is that I should speak to Thee through Thee, than that I should speak to myself without Thee.'

He said, 'Now give ear to the Law, and transgress not My commands and forbiddings, that thy strivings may earn Our thanks.'

I said, 'Insomuch as I profess the faith and my heart firmly believes, if Thou givest thanks, it is better that Thou shouldst thank Thyself rather than Thy slave; and if Thou blamest, Thou art pure of all fault.'

He said, 'From whom didst thou learn?'

I said, 'He who asks this question knows better than he who is asked; for He is both the Desired and the Desirer, the Answered and the Answerer.'

When He had perceived the purity of my inmost soul, then my soul heard a shout of God's satisfaction; He sealed me with His good pleasure. He illuminated me, and delivered me out of the darkness of the carnal soul and the foulnesses of the fleshly nature. I knew that through Him I lived; and of His bounty I spread the carpet of gladness in my heart.

He said, 'Ask whatsoever thou wilt.'

I said, 'I wish for Thee, for Thou art more excellent than bounty, greater than generosity, and through Thee I have found content in Thee. Since Thou art mine, I have rolled up the scroll of beauty and generosity. Keep me not from Thee, and proffer not before me that which is inferior to Thee.'

For a while He did not answer me. Then, laying the crown of munificence on my head, He spoke.

'Truth thou speakest, and reality thou seekest, in that thou hast seen the truth and heard the truth.'

I said, 'If I have seen, through Thee I have seen, and if I have heard, through Thee I have heard. First Thou heardest, then I heard.'

And I uttered many phrases to Him. Consequently He gave me wings of majesty, so that I flew in the arenas of His glory and beheld the wonders of His handiwork. Perceiving my weakness and recognizing my need, He strengthened me with His own strength and arrayed me with His own adornment. He laid the crown of munificence on my head, and opened unto me the door of the palace of Unity.

Unity is a rare state but it must become permanent by repeated occurrence. Inherent in this permanency is certainty (*yaqin*), the state of assurance (*nafs e mutmaina*), the self which is certain. In the unitary experience of Abu-Yazid, we notice the feeling of certainty. In other words, with the occurrence of *reza* (self-satisfaction) within the experience of unity one feels certain of the completeness of the path. Certainty (*yaqin*) is the culmination of all the stages and *ahwal* (states) which one has gone through. It is self-evident, joyous, and like sunshine it is its own proof. One feels it in one's marrow, and manifests it by clear vision. In fact, one becomes a vision and demonstrates it: a vision which is full of wisdom and manifests the light of the path for the future as well as expressing the past. According to Sufism even the state of certainty is not a bound state. It is an open end, and one can still make progress and go from the state of *ain al yaqin*, that is, the essence of certainty to the reality of certainty (*haq al yaqin*) and finally to *ilm al-yaqin*, that is, knowing certainty.

This knowledge is not like knowledge which is learned from instruction. It is experiential, vision-like, full of wisdom and occurs with total certainty where the speaker has a vision and its instrument is *intuition*. All master Sufis have noted this ability. In fact, it is one of the major signs of one's re-integration, though it is a beginning, and thus intuition has a range which begins from the natural unitary vision of a child to sudden insight of an inventor – to revelation of a prophet. The reality of intuition as a man's faculty is clear in the following passage by

Rumi, a concept which also appeared in the writings of Ibn-e-Sina, the great physician of the golden age of Islam. Rumi declared:[6]

> *Intelligence consists of two intelligences; the former is the*
> *acquired one which you learn like a boy at school.*
> *From book and teacher and reflection and [commiting to]*
> *memory, and from*
> *Concepts and from excellent and virgin [hitherto unstudied]*
> *sciences.*
> *[By this means] your intelligence becomes superior to that of*
> *others;*
> *but through preserving [retaining in your mind] that knowledge*
> *you are heavily burdened.*
> *You [occupied] in wandering and going about [in search of*
> *knowledge] are a preserving [recording] tablet,*
> *The preserved tablet is he that passed by and this.*
> *The other intelligence is the gift of God: its foundation is in*
> *the midst of the soul.*
> *When the water of God-given knowledge gushes from the*
> *breast, it does not become fetid or old or yellow*
> *And if its way of issue [to the outside] be stopped,*
> *What harm?*
> *For it gushes continually from the house [of the heart].*
> *The acquired intelligence is like to conduits which*
> *run into a house from the street;*
> *[If] its [the house's] waterway is blocked, it is without*
> *[water].*
> *Seek the fountain from within yourself!*

The reality of this dynamic force of 'intuition' which makes life overflowing, a surprise at each experience, helps one regain a new vitality to discover the inner life by illumination of 'name', 'attributes', and 'essence'. Thus, we have passed through the path from where we gained our conviction to the point of birth and intuition, giving full coverage where vertical growth ends and infinite horizons for the climax of experience, known as *An*, begins.

Chapter 7
The hierarchy of Sufi personality

Sufism is an open-ended order. Its horizon is infinity, and from there beyond. What we have discussed may seem to some individuals like the end of the journey, but it is merely a beginning. I have already given some idea of the relativeness of the Sufi state. Indeed, the great Sufi, Jalalalddin Rumi declared that the rule in Sufism is that everyone should progress according to his or her own capacity and understanding. Similarly the activity of 'insight' reveals varying degrees of qualitative depth among different Sufis. In fact, the degree of illumination reveals their vertical intensity and horizontal comprehension. If we take this measure as an index of the hierarchy of Sufis we will find that at the bottom of the scale there were those early purified Muslims who maintained perfect faith. These early Sufis had God's image constantly in mind and heart – an image which they manifested in behaviour and action. According to Hujwiri in *Kashf al-Mahjub* the early Sufi, Muhammad Ibn Wasi was reported to have said:[1] 'I never saw anything without seeing God therein' (i.e. through perfect faith).

However, it should be noted that this group used the demonstration method when they referred to 'seeing'. They actually saw the act with their eyes, for they were involved with created things, not with the essence of creation. Another authority, Niffari, describes this elementary level among Sufis:[2] 'God said to me, "The least of the sciences of nearness is that you should see in everything the effects of beholding Me, and that this vision should prevail over you more than your gnosis of Me." ' In interpreting this passage Nicholson adds:[3]

He [Niffari] means that the least of the sciences of nearness (proximity to God) is that when you look at anything, sensibly or intellectually or otherwise, you should be conscious of beholding God with a vision clearer than your vision of that thing. There are diverse degrees in this matter. Some mystics say that they never see anything without seeing God before it. Others say, 'without seeing God after it,' or 'with it'; or they say that they see nothing but God. A certain Sufi said, 'I made the pilgrimage and saw the Ka'ba, but not the Lord of the Ka'ba'. This is the perception of one who is veiled. Then he said, 'I made the pilgrimage again, and I saw both the Ka'ba and the Lord of the Ka'ba'. This is contemplation of the Self-subsistence through which everything subsists, i.e. he saw the Ka'ba subsisting through the Lord of the Ka'ba. Then he said, 'I made the pilgrimage a third time, and saw the Lord of the Ka'ba, but not the Ka'ba.' This is the 'station' of *waqfat* (passing-away in the essence). In the present case the author is referring to contemplation of the Self-subsistence.

Perhaps these categories can be related to three types of objects of desire. They are: (1) the *shaikh*, the Sufi master and passing beyond him; (2) identification with God, and finally with (3) the essence of creation, that is love, the process of creation. In short:

1 Personification
2 Deification
3 'Unification' (with the essence; 'loyalty to life')

Personification, that is, becoming like one's own father, teacher, craft master, and guide, is one of the common 'processes of growth' in every culture. In Persian culture it was a strong mechanism of cultural preservation.

Traditionally, in Persia, identification has been a mechanism for assimilating the qualities that one respects, values that one idealizes. The two basic qualities of human nature, intense desire and ideation of certain images, are at work in the process of human identification, and they eventually force a receptive seeker to break away from his previous attachment and unify with his object of desire (guide or master). Such a process in its elementary form was most strikingly apparent in the relationship of the master to the apprentice, both in professional and in religious life. The apprentice not only learned a trade while being associated with the master, but in continued association with him, he formed an image of the master which he retained for a long time. In this process he became accustomed to a pattern of life which gave him a limited but integrated personality. In Sufism as in the guild system this very mechanism of growth was in work, and the early Sufis sought the ideal within their masters.

This process of identification with the master, while it was a beginning for great Sufis such as Rumi, in the process of his identification with Shams; for some other Sufis this stage sufficed, at least as long as the master lived. A striking example of this process of identification with the master is recorded by the late Professor Macdonald in *The Religious Attitude and Life in Islam* concerning the process of inner growth of Towakul Beg, a disciple of Molla-Shah. Professor Macdonald paraphrases Towakul Beg's narrative:[4]

> He [the master] made me sit before him, my senses being as though intoxicated, and ordered me to reproduce my own image within myself; and, after having bandaged my eyes, he asked me to concentrate all my mental faculties on my heart. I obeyed, and in an instant, by the divine favour and by the spiritual assistance of the Sheykh, my heart opened. I saw, then, that there was something like an overturned cup within me. This having been set upright, a sensation of unbounded happiness filled my being. I said to the master: 'This cell where I am seated before you – I see a faithful reproduction of it within me, and it appears to me as though another Tawakkul Beg were seated before another Molla-Shah.' He replied, 'Very good! The first apparition which appears to thee is the image of the master.' He then ordered me to uncover my eyes; and I saw him, with the physical organ of vision, seated before me. He then made me bind my eyes again, and I perceived him with my spiritual sight, seated similarly before me. Full of astonishment, I cried out, 'O Master! whether I look with my physical organs or with my spiritual sight, always it is you that I see!'

Of course, this single incident did not result in the transformation of Towakul Beg. To Molla-Shah, the real transformation, that is, departing entirely from one's own past experience (*fana*) and being reborn within the world of experience of the master was a gradual act and often took over ten years, culminating in a state of mind where the disciple experienced the master as

God-like and saw him in everything with which he came in contact. One of the clearest cases of this identification occurred in Rumi's identification with Shams, when he composed the following lyric:[5]

When I talk of chiefs, he is the Master, when
I search the heart he is the beloved, when
I seek peace he is the mediator, when
I come to the battlefield, he is the dagger, when
I attend a party, he is the wine and comfit, when
I go into the rose garden, he is elegant.
When I go into the mine he is the cornelian and ruby, when
I go into the sea he is the pearl. When
I am on the plains he is the garden rose; when
I come to the Heaven he is the star. When
I come to the upper ranks he is the pinnacle, when
I burn out of sorrow he is the censer. When
I prepare to fight in time of battle, he is
*   both the officer on duty and the general; when*
I come to a feast in time of joy, he is the cupbearer, the
*   minstrel and the cup. When*
I write a letter to the beloved, he is the ink, the
*   inkwell and the paper; when*
I awaken he is my intelligence. When
I go to sleep, he is my dream; when
I search for a rhyme in a lyric, he is the
*   rhyme-giver in my memory.*
Whatever image that you think of
He, like a painter, is the brush in the hand.
If you still look for a superior
He is better than 'better'.
Go, leave speech and book, for
It is far better that he be the book.
Be silent, for all six sides are his light
And when you pass these six sides, there he is —
*   the Judge.*

At other stages, Shams became Rumi's pain and remedy, his

carrier to truth, and always his 'God' and his everlasting life. Once more I would like to remind the reader that even in this process of identification with the *Shaikh*, the principle of relativity was essential. The ratio between the capacity of the seeker and the degree of the master's state was important. There were situations where the master was so perfect in self-hood that the Sufi seeker had to spend years to arrive at the state of the master. Such a master Sufi was Shams, who as a perfect man remained Jalalalddin Rumi's image for years, even though Rumi himself was a great master. In other cases, a Sufi seeker might reach such a spiritual state that he made an impact even on his master's state. One such case was the relationship between Ala' udellin 'Attar, a master Sufi, and one of his disciples known as Khamush. On occasions Khamush intentionally interfered with the master's state of psyche – a situation which eventually caused their separation.

Deification

Though the Sufi seekers often considered their master as the personification of God, some gradually deviated from the master's image in order to know the creator directly. Whereas the first group of Sufi seekers, as we previously described, sought an insight into created things, strived, and patiently waited for illumination which might lead them to the state of the master; the second group directly, or via a journey through the state of the master, concentrated on union with God as He had revealed Himself in the Qur'an. A classic example of this process of identification is expressed in Shaikh 'Attar's allegorical tale of *Mantiq ul Tair* (*The Conference of the Birds*). By means of the allegory, 'Attar tries to convey how, among thousands of seekers (the birds resembling Sufi seekers), only a handful, in fact only thirty, become God Himself. Or more specifically, through the process of purification, the seeker illuminates his whole being to the extent that he becomes one with God. 'Attar summarizes this union thus:[6]

And if they looked at both together, both were
The Simurgh (*a name both for the seeker and sought*), *neither*
    more nor less.
This one was that, and that one this; the like
Of this hath no one heard in the world.

Likewise al-Hallaj believed that true prayer is feeling one
with God, not submitting to Him. And when he confidently
achieved this state he declared: 'Thy Spirit is mingled in my
spirit even as wine is mingled with pure water. When anything
touches Thee, it touches me. Lo in every case Thou art I!'[7]

On another occasion, al-Hallaj described his state as follows:[8]

I am He whom I love, and He whom I love is I:
We are two spirits dwelling in one body.
If thou seest me, thou seest Him,
And if thou seest Him, thou seest us both.

In a similar manner we have already discussed the deification
of Bayazid. However, before explaining this process of transcendance, I would like to further clarify the process of personal
deification, which is based on the innumerable attributes of
God as they appear in the Qur'an. A Sufi could identify with
one of these attributes or with several, or with all. This process
was called *hulyl*, that is, infusion of God's attributes, or attributes within the state of the Sufi. It has also been discussed in
terms of *fana fel al Allah*, that is, passing away in God's existence,
as well as simply, identification of the Sufi with divine being,
known as union (*itihad* or *itasal*, or *jam*). Whatever name we
use, the process was the same, and it required: (1) intensive
concentration (*tawaja*); (2) assimilation of the attributes of the
qualities, will, and desires of the 'object of desire', whatever
that object might be; (3) stabilization of this state in a way
that the infusion of wills would take place, such that one could
claim as al-Hallaj did:[9]

Thy will be done, O my lord and master!
Thy will be done, O my purpose and meaning!
O essence of my being, O goal of my desire,

O my speech and my hints and my gestures!
O all of my all, O my hearing and my sight,
O my whole and my elements and my particles!

Unification with life's essence

Unification with the life essence is recognition of deification in
everything. However, further transformation could still take
place as the Sufi seeker gradually, through identification with
various attributes, transcended the duality of subject and
object. Such a one was Abu Said Ibn Abi 'l Khayr, who in
experiencing union with the essence, said:[10]

I am love, I am beloved; no less am I the lover.
I am the mirror and I am the beauty,
Therefore behold me in myself.

At this state there has taken place: eradication of names (such
as relating to *ka'ba*, cross, crescent), elimination of group
affiliation (such as being a Turk, Persian, or Arab, Jew, Muslim,
or Zoroastrian), and disappearance of concepts (such as East,
West, paradise, hell) – in short, relatedness to time and place.
One exists within the realm of the beloved, and manifests oneself in terms of the mechanism of 'love'. The Sufi is now able
to practise the art of love which exists in the depth of the psyche,
below the surface of the cultural reality of 'name', and beneath
the reality of attributes. It is this practice of the 'art of loving'
which the Sufis attribute to the creator and created things,
and thereby help us make the discovery that creation turns on
the wheel of love. Such a gradual tendency takes place within
the essence of man and brings him to a state which the poet
Sa'di found himself in when he said, 'I am in love with the
whole Cosmos, because the whole Cosmos originated from one
existence'; or as expressed by Rumi, who after years of residing
in the safety of Shams's existence (the God-head), finally.
transcended it and declared, 'I am born twice, once through
Shams, another time through love.'

Love then becomes the 'drug of all drugs'. The mechanism of creation becomes love, for as Jalalalddin Rumi claimed, people often claim that they make love, while they overlook the fact that they were born out of love. Not only man but minerals, the organic and the inorganic world, are constantly changing on the basis of love. Love changes thorns into beautiful roses, vinegar into wine, misfortune to good fortune, slave to ruler, grief to joy, and illness to health.

It is here that Sufi thought has made a great contribution, and unlike Darwin, Freud and Marx, whose doctrines were all based on the principles of conflict, Sufism experientially discovered and proved that the greatest mediator of rational and irrational conflicts in man, society and history was *love*. In fact, the Sufis advise us indirectly that if a dispute, or a social or personal ill cannot be remedied through reason and laws (as in today's world), then hand it to *love*, the greatest compassionate and caretaker of all, and examine its wonderful results. The music of the Cosmos gradually becomes the music of love. However, it has to come slowly, and one must discover and become aware that one's 'cosmic memory' has had many encounters with *love*, which must be brought to light slowly. Amid such a gradual concentration on the creation and past, and discovering the everlasting force of love, one comes to realize that, except for intense love, no other task or activity becomes worth while. One discovers that 'servitude is a chain, lordship a headache. But love leads to an everlasting life and its succession a happy life.'

In this final state the Sufi seeker may first long for the appearance of 'love' as a function of life, if not identical with it. Like Rumi, the seeker may learn a lesson about the universe from the conduct of lovers and discover that in nature and culture forms may be different, but the process is the same. Creation is born out of love. As the seeker becomes a firm believer of the mechanism of 'love', he may bow to it and attribute to it innumerable powers. He may discover it as the 'physician of all ills', the remedy for man's pride and vanity; he may perceive that it was through love that Moses fell in a swoon on

Mount Sinai, through love that Christ became the 'Spirit of God', and Muhammad became the intimate friend of God (*Habib al Allah*). He may discover that Moses' burning of the bush, Muhammad's luminous hands, and Christ's life-giving hands all resulted from the intensity and impact of love on their organism. It is due to this quality of love that all master Sufis considered the religion of love far superior to ordinary belief. Love as a religion is different from all other creeds; it reduces division and brings about unity between human beings, because religion basically arises from the human situation which requires an object of love outside the human soul. Love is the real response to that natural urge; it is colourless, and an inspiration causing form and creative patterns. When Rumi finally found that love is the real guide, he expressed his boundless love for all:

> *I gave up all means and ambition and fortune;*
> *I purchased love of humanity. How can I remain without gifts.*

When Abu Said discovered love, he claimed it as a natural creed of man:[11]

> *He whom destiny places among the group of lovers,*
> *He becomes free from mosque and church.*
> *He whose mode of life is passed away in love, he has*
> *no dogma, no belief, no gnosis, nor [conventional] religion.*

In like manner, Hafiz, in the following verse, repeatedly begs his audience to put aside prejudiced sects, abandon the legend, and discover the truth:

> *Leave aside the battle of seventy-two sects,*
> *For just as their followers did not know the truth,*
> *So too, they themselves made up legends.*

Thus, in Sufism, truth and love become identical and the former arises from the latter (union). Because union requires selflessness, Hafiz and other master Sufis concluded that love is denied to selfish persons, whether it is the result of self-seeking impulses (*nafs*), power, wealth, or servitude to man.

However, once more practice and action is emphasized so that one's nature will be moulded in the process of union – love. This 'art of loving' must be practised and must involve one totally until one can, like Jalalalddin Rumi, hear its melody constantly:[12]

> Save the melody of love, whatever
> Melody I heard in the world
> Was the noisy drum.

The Sufi tastes love in everything which goes through his senses; and it becomes its own proof, just as the sun is its own proof. It must become discernible within the heart and clear as a mechanism of human relations or as an epistomological theory of knowing. Love is a genuine experience of man in his relatedness to nature and man. It is this intensive unending relation which produces creative vision, instantaneous knowledge and a wisdom which is far superior to intellectual achievement.

Further intensity of this 'love' has created the revelation as it has appeared in God's messengers. It is an amazing act of creation that all three major prophets – Moses, Christ, and Muhammad were fatherless; they all related to their mother's love. They all sought to uncover the mystery of the absent father, and when they did not discover it in man, they discovered it in the eternal father, in the love-pulsation of the universe, which revealed to them 'revelations' in terms of holy books.

Thus, the hierarchy of the Sufis begins with the seekers who pass through stages, illuminating themselves through the experience of various states. They ranked lowest among the Sufis until they became thoroughly identified with their own master; they then became the chosen Sufi, just as the ordinary Sufis were the chosen ones in their community. These elect Sufis were chosen according to their power, controlling spiritual illumination and remaining in that luminous state. In other words, as I mentioned in Chapter 2, the Sufis strived to achieve *waqt e khosh* – the moment of illumination and natural intoxication. The elect Sufis known as *wali* (the intimate of God) were also known as *aba al waqt*, that is, those who create the *waqt e khosh* at will. Such a Sufi has the grace of God and his will is His, and he is thereby bestowed with the secrets of the world. Nicholson masterfully explains it thus:[13]

> The inspiration of the Islamic saints, though verbally distinguished from that of the prophets and inferior in degree, is of the same kind. In consequence of their intimate relation to God, the veil shrouding the supernatural, or, as a Moslem would say, the unseen world, from their perceptions is withdrawn at intervals, and in their fits of ecstasy they rise to the prophetic level. Neither deep learning in divinity, nor devotion to good works, nor asceticism nor moral purity makes the Mohammedan a saint; he may have all or none of these things, but the only indispensable qualification is that ecstasy and rapture which is the outward sign of 'passing away' from the phenomenal self. Anyone thus encaptured (*Majdhub*) is a *Wali*, and when such persons are recognized through their power of working miracles, they are venerated as saints not only after death but also during their lives.

Even the saints had their own order and hierarchy. The most eminent one was the *Qutb* (axis) of the historical epoch. Ranked below him according to one authority, Hujuiri, were various grades: *Akhyar* (the good doers), followed by *Abdals* (the substitutes), and then *Abrars* (the pious ones), *Awtud* (the supporters), and finally at the bottom, *Nuqaba* (the overseers).

The miracle of a saint was not as intense as that of a prophet and it was thus known as *karamat*, in contrast to the Prophet's miracle, *mujizat*. In other words, we should remind ourselves of the unknown dark room of the psyche and the candles: the illumination of the Prophet illuminated the past, present and future, while the experience of illumination of the saint was less radiant.

A hierarchy existed in still another dimension, where three categories of illumination were taking place. The lowest type of illumination was the illumination of names, that is, the cultural phenomenon. Through the process of illumination of 'name' one arrived at the state of objects with certain qualities, such that the Sufi was no longer aware of words. A little story which also has social significance may illustrate the case:

The story goes that a Persian, a Turk, an Arab and a Greek were travelling together. They found a gold coin and all of them wanted to buy grapes. The Persian said that he wanted '*angur*', the Turk, '*uzum*', the Arab, '*inab*', and the Greek '*istafil*'. A quarrel ensued as a result of their lack of understanding of one another's language. Fortunately a multilingual passer-by inquired about the cause of the quarrel. They each told him the story in their own language. Having heard them all, the passer-by pulled a few 'grapes' out of his market basket, and conveyed to them the fact that they all wanted the same thing but were expressing it in different tongues. Then he advised them, 'Pass on from the name and look at the attributes in order that they may show you the way to the essence.' In other words, the illumination of qualities occurs at a deeper level of experience. Through the illumination of qualities one arrives at the common denominator of all qualities, such as waves, lights and sounds. The countable becomes countless.

Of greater importance, however, is the illumination of the essence. Chemical elements and physical qualities appear as the world of attributes, but if by chance we discover that 'mother element', which has produced all other elements, then we get to the world of essence. The bridge between the illumination of essence and the attributes is the illumination of all matter. One often experiences it naturally without being aware of those processes. These particular experiences when added together, that is, through emptying the mind, produce an illumination of the total life situation; in other words, one becomes enlightened. Through concentration, every intelligent person can remove the 'name' from an object and arrive at a concrete situation, even arrive at the invisible phenomenon behind the forces – the fluid composition of the material, but it is the illumination of the essence which one must unfold. However, even insight into the process of happiness can contribute to the creation of greater happiness, that is, it facilitates our experience of union with the object of desire. It is this experience of union which eliminates the duality of subject and object, seer and seen, lover and beloved, instantaneously with a flash and creates new awareness.

Al-Gillani (fourteenth century) advocated a type of inner evolution. He called the essence which is separate from all qualities and names, the 'dark mist' (al'-ama), whereas Rumi refers to it simply as 'essence'. Iqbal in his *Development o Metaphysics in Persia* compares al'-ama to the modern concept of the unconscious. According to al-Gillani the al'-ama develops consciousness by passing through various evolutions, specifically: the world of unity, form, and name. In this process the simple essence appears as subject and object, and the world of many comes into being, that is, a whole series of being appear. Name and attributes are given to this world of many. The 'one', the essence, the 'dark mist' remain constant, but the many change. Opposites must be reconciled and at last united, the many must again become one. Al-Gillani succinctly described this dual reality metaphorically by saying that water becomes ice and then water once more. The essence is water; through inner change it takes the form of ice; then again it becomes water. Thus the essence which is crystallized in the world of names and attributes seeks to return to its reality. Man is the most remarkable thing, for in man all attributes are united and the essence finds itself completely realized. When he deciphers his essence, form and essence become harmonized and he is one with the universe. In short, al-Gillani believed that in the process of the art of self-liberation of Sufism, a Sufi must go from the state of 'I-ness', to 'He-ness', to 'one-ness', where 'I-ness', is the state of personification, 'He-ness', the state of deification and 'one-ness', the state of unity of all things. In my own simple terms, one must arrive at a zero-point (nothingness) so that one will be able to make everything meaningful and joyous. In this process one has developed a pure organic system.

In conclusion, the impact of the process of Sufism on self-decipherment is enormous. It relates mainly to the period when Adam was not yet created, as well as to infinity in the future, and it makes both aspects meaningful. Evidence tells me that one's system will change including the substances in his blood. There are innumerable evidences in Sufism regarding the personality structure of the great masters. We know that their endurance, patience, physiological system, their voice, and artistic abilities were extraordinary. Their magnetism could even control wild beasts; their warm feelings enriched whoever came in contact with them; they cured the incurable; their concentration moved external bodies, as Al-Ghazzali observed: 'While others (non-Sufis) moved themselves, the Sufis moved external bodies and influenced them without moving.'

Though the personality change of novice Sufis moving through the path has not been measured scientifically, I am confident that even the chemical composition of their body changes after this experience. Here it is helpful to make some remarks about the physiological transcendence of Zen Buddhists, who were studied in recent years by the late Professor Sato and his colleague Professor Akishige. At the founding meeting of the Union of Asian Psychology in Tokyo in August 1972, Professor Akishige reported on his findings:[14]

Scientific research has shown that during Zen practice the respiration curve and plethysmogram show regular rhythmical patterns, and in comparison with inhalation, exhalation is obviously longer. The oxygen consumption decreases and the partial pressures of gases in the blood change, leading to various changes in visceral responses. That is, to say, the acid-base balance and high or low blood pressure which had been disturbed by various causes are normalized. Cerebral blood flow decreases and systematic blood flow increases to produce a desirable body condition. The metabolic rate drops below the basal metabolic rate. All these factors taken together suggest that the respiratory-cardiovascular system keeps a more desirable rate of dynamic equilibrium while in Zen practice than in other situations.
    ... Close scientific research using electroencephalogram, galvanic skin response, skin resistance, verbal reports and others indicate that the mental state while in Zen practice is not dim, nor is there distraction; it is a very clear, awakened state which continues stationary. There is no sign of verbal conflict, and complete peace of mind is produced. Thus, it evidently differs from the hypnotic trance state. . . .

What, then is behind Zen practice? It is the doctrine of non-ego or the thought of 'nothingness' which denies any fixed standpoint. Zogen Zen, which was perfected in Japan, denies even the seeking for enlightenment, for enlightenment is not a thing to be gained by 'Zagen' as a means – it already exists in 'Zagen' as an end in itself. Hence practice and enlightenment are not two things but one. Enlightenment is not something to seek in the future; people are already at this moment in the world of enlightenment though they are not awakened to the fact. Since in the world of Zen there are no dualistic ideas, there is no reason for conflict of ideology. And the way of Zen will bring an end to struggles in the world and bring happiness to all mankind.

Finally, these recent scientific studies on Asian psychology indicate that the trend of Western psychology is towards this ultra-psychological system which makes living vital, limtis the process of ageing as we know it, and makes life meaningful to the end, when death becomes a window to a new form of life.

Chapter 8
An; creative moment: the climax of Sufi being

Introduction

My basic premise, as I tried to state in the Introduction, is that the root of man's religious, philosophical, scientific and artistic knowledge is creative experience. In fact what differentiates man from beast is his creative vision. It is the formation of creative vision and objectivization of form which expands consciousness. The real definition of man's joy and happiness is nothing but experiencing creative moments; the permanency of this joy depends upon transforming it into consciousness and retaining this level of awareness. The moment of creative experience is so real, so genuine, so vital that we often give up our possessions for its actualization and sacrifice our material comforts for its manifestation. Such an experience happens to men regardless of time, place and the degree of culture. In fact it is the common denominator of all mankind. It is characterized by action for the sake of action, for the sake of the beloved, for the sake of someone, or some ideals outside of ourselves. It is self-explanatory, self-directing, self-forming and self-expanding. It is known by different names – Goethe calls it *entelechy;* Coleridge, *imagination creatix;* Galileo, *illume naturale;* Whitehead, *prehension;* Eastern authorities *te,* the unthinkable ingenuity, illumination, knowing without trying, just being there, union, moment of instant birth and rebirth, existential moment; the Greeks, *Kairos* (the auspicious moment); and the Sufis,[1] *An* (moment of good fortune). However, it makes no difference by what name we identify it. It is the *experience* which matters, not its cultural signs and symbols. We know that the essence of every culture, every life, is such an illuminating experience. Though its process cannot easily be recreated, numerous examples exist. In this chapter I shall identify these genuine experiences of man as they have appeared in Sufism.

An: an explanation

The existential Persian concept *An* is difficult to define; its meaning is best conveyed by analogy. It is said that if one steps on a Persian carpet at exactly 3.00 a.m. it will fly; but such good fortune is fleeting, for the person invariably steps on the carpet an instant (*An*) before or after 3.00 a.m. This idea of a precise instant, the real time in transcendental and ex periential psychology of enlightened Persians, undoubtedly resembles the idea of *Kairos* in Greek mythology.

When I contemplated further on the concept of *Kairos* and compared it with the notion of *An* in Persian culture, I found that both are of an intensive character rather than extensive, both are spaceless and both are the culmination of a variety of apparent and inapparent factors. In Greek mythology, *Kairos* personifies opportunity: in transcendental Persian psychology the opportune time, the fortunate time, is often mentioned and a common everyday greeting is '*Khoshvaght Bashid*' (let it be a fortunate time). This greeting has its origin in the expressions of the Sufis who sought enlightenment. Clearly related to the concept of *Kairos* as a symbol of total existence requiring confrontation and the occurrence of events at an exact moment is the Sufi concept that the enlightened Sufi must seek the 'right time', the real moment, that is, the instant of total relatedness.

These similarities encouraged me to consider two other terms which were used to identify Sufis in Persian literature. They were called either *Ibn al Vaght* (The Child of the Moment) or *Abu al Vaght* (The Father of the Moment). However, I believe that these two expressions were actually used to identify two different states of the psyche among Persians who sought *An*. The expression *Ibn al Vaght* (The Child of the Moment) referred to the state of the less experienced Sufis, that is, those who had to wait, meditate and concentrate in order that the moment of joy, union, and relatedness would appear to them. But the expression *Abu al Vaght* was reserved for the highest rank of enlightenment of a Master Sufi who could create the moment, or more precisely, his psyche had become so receptive that certain ordinary signs could relate him to cosmic joy – to ecstasy. For example, Sufi scholars relate that one day Mowlana Jalalalddin Rumi, a Master Sufi of the thirteenth century,[2] passed through the goldsmiths' quarter of the bazaar and heard the gentle tapping of a jeweller, who was himself a notable Sufi. The gentle sound stimulated ('tuned in') Mowlana and he began a whirling dance which ended in a great ecstasy of several hours.

What this event means is that a great master can relate human and non-human signs to their original essence and correctly relate the ordinary signs to a deeper layer of communication. In other words, *Abu al Vaght*, a great Master Sufi, possesses a more sensitive organic 'antenna' than the *Ibn al Vaght* Sufi. The one needs preparation for the occurrence of *An*, while the other is almost *An* itself. *Abu al Vaght* has greater control of the situation to bring together not-being and being, the *Ibn al Vaght* less control. In contemporary speech it might be said that *Abu al Vaght* needs no stimulus to tune in, whereas *Ibn al Vaght* requires a greater concentration for the birth of magnetism of his psyche. One is more sensitive than the other; one more receptive than the other; one possesses a greater number of symbols by which he can harmonize his psyche to the motion of the universe; the other less. One has had more original experience and is multi-dimensional, whereas the other has less control of the occurrence of mystical experience. One is like a shining mirror, the other a dusty one. One is the subject of time, the other the object of chance.

These two expressions, *Abu al Vaght* and *Ibn al Vaght* also serve to reactivate the issue of temporal and eternal time which philosophers have dealt with. There is no doubt that both in *An* and in Greek *Kairos* timing is essential; but which time? What is the difference between fortunate, exact and ordinary time?

When I was reading about *Kairos* and the concepts of temporal and eternal time, the concept of Bergson's time as 'duration' passed through my mind, followed in quick succession by the physicist's concept of time, the so-called 'time zones' of Standard Time, and the heightened argument of Islamic philosophers on time. I recalled that the scholastics considered 'time' as an imaginary thing, philosophers thought that it was brought about by the revolution of the planets in the heavens and some Sufis considered 'time' to be without beginning or end. They likened it to a container in which creation and annihilation take place. Creation and annihilation take place in one breath; before and after, past and future are mental.

Finally, I conclude that *An* is the moment of fulfilment; it is an instant of birth and rebirth, awareness and transcending experience, new experience, relatedness, union and joy. Such a moment, *An*, appears when 'temporal' time transcends itself and arrives at 'eternal' time; that is, when not-being in the form of successions of events, appear one after another and touch the shore of being. When 'I' becomes identical with 'not-I' and when the personal becomes the universal, we can then eliminate the usual dualistic concept of time, which has consumed the energy of a large number of theologians and philosophers in the past. This developmental concept of time provides us with an opportunity to give: (1) an organic theory of time; (2) identify it with 'events', action which generates and creates a succession of actions until it unfolds in terms of *An* or manifests creative moment. It also provides us with an opportunity to differentiate between the imitative moments of others and the experiential moment of our own life and thereby discover that cultural (arbitrary, imitative) events are only significant in the sense that we arrive at the point that if cultural events limited to temporal time mature sufficiently they will transcend themselves and give us inner freedom in eternal time. In other words, intelligence is temporal and grows into wisdom which is eternal; reason gives birth to 'intuition', discipline to total freedom, form to formlessness, individuality to universality, personality to humanity, and societal to cosmological. No doubt, the peak of the transcendental experience and the common denominator of various forms (religious, scientific, artistic, humanistic) is the 'creative moment', which again is the outer expression of *An* or the instant at which temporal time like a drop disappears in the current of eternity.

On the basis of my recent work, *Creativity and Human Development*,[3] I have also come to believe that the creative moment in scientists, founders of religions, artists, and original thinkers all appear when intellect has exhausted itself, when formalistic religion has lost its effectivity, when the artist has become discipline itself, and when the thinkers have assimilated and consumed at least one system of thought. In such a state and suddenly at a moment when the psyche has regained its total harmony and is free from internal conflict, then instantly an original vision appears. That moment is *An*.

Anatomy of *An*: the creative moment

The nature of *An* is so comprehensive and at the same time so intangible that it is hard to define. Perhaps that is why the great Master Sufis resorted to similes, comparing *An* to a sharp sword which cuts off the past from the future. In other words, *An* is total presence, it 'is' itself. It has also been compared to the instant when a fish appears on the surface then disappears. This simile makes better sense when we recall that Rumi the Master Sufi viewed the whole psyche as an ocean in which every type of being exists; then certain favourable waves bring one of the living creatures to the surface.[4] Iqbal considers the state of 'I am-ness' a manifestation of *An* and as the highest state in the rank of selfhood.[5] In our own time, Carl Rogers, the psychologist, has coined the state of 'isness',[6] and it is also known to us that in the Old Testament, God told Moses that 'I am that I am', and Abraham the Prophet also expressed his state in terms of 'I am'.

More than a decade ago when I spontaneously composed the poem, 'Here I am', I was not fully aware of the psychological significance of 'I-amness'.[7] The 'I-amness', the product of *An*, is undoubtedly the result of the union of subject and object, which I have also discussed in my unitary theory of happiness and creativity[8] as the great moment when knower and known become one in a way that one internally experiences happiness (the inner expression of *An*) and externally notices the relatedness of subject and object in a new light. In Sufism the unitary experience is known as *Ita-sal* (union), the result of which has been expressed in terms of inspiration (al-Ghazzali),[9] the removal of the veil (Rumi and others),[10] comparable to the modern concept of emotional and cultural blocks, illumination (al-Shadhili),[11] transcendence of the cosmic crypt (Ibn Sina)[12] and a moment of joy (Khayyam).[13]

Again, it should be noted that in attitude Sufis were relativists and believed in various types of inspiration, illumination and inner joy; but this relativity was cumulative and led to the climax of truth – an experience in *An*. They also categorized the states of the psyche by showing that the lowest degree of sensitivity requires external motive power for inspiration. The external object of inspiration can be any type of object. It depends upon the state of the seeker, and the highest state of the Sufi did not require external stimuli for inspiration because he had already become the inspired one.

Therefore when *An* occurs it is self-explanatory. The Sufis claimed that the sun with all its brightness needs no proof – the sun is its own proof; so too is *An*. Another characteristic of *An* is that it illuminates its own future course; it is also self-directive. In this sense it is therefore complimentary to the organic sphere of life. It obviously opens up a new course for human growth in which the guides and educators create the condition in which the seekers can experience events, the accumulation of which produces what we have defined as a moment of deeper 'awareness', a type of insight which can direct the course of life and provide a climax of being.

Furthermore, it is not necessary or practical that man experiences *An* every day or regularly, because an experience of *An* by its very nature is a great potentiality. It can be expanded and produced in innumerable forms. In other words, the experience which manifests itself in *An*, that is the vision, is pregnant and serves as a 'mother idea'. It should be given form; otherwise, it will remain separate from the personality structure. The formation of the product of *An* forms the character of the seeker, alleviates mental maladies and improves health. Perhaps on the basis of this finding we can conclude that the best type of education is experiential, the best type of therapy occupational therapy, and the best type of life an active one. Of course, as Rumi asserted, one must always keep in mind that each experience of *An* is like one rung of a ladder and one must not remain on any one step,[14] that is, any one transitional state. It is through the formation of a product of *An* that one can experience still a more intensive state of *An*. What is essential then, as we shall see below, is the succession of events wherein the arrival of one *An* follows the fulfilment of another. In this sense the experience of *An* is an inner evolution of the psyche and can be compared to layers of an onion which originate from the core and extend out until the core is related to the outer world, or like unfolding circles which appear when a pebble is thrown into a pool or calm lake. If there is no interference, the smaller circles widen out and lead to larger ones until they touch the shore. Perhaps 'experience' in *An* is the link between generations and manifests the inner evolution of man.

To my knowledge, no one has given us a more comprehensive view of this spiritual evolution than Farid al Din 'Attar, the pharmacist and Sufi of the twelfth century. In his masterwork, *The Book of Creative Suffering*, 'Attar takes man (the primitive man before Adam) as a seeker. All of humanity is perceived as one body ascending from the primitive seeker. Original man, like twentieth-century man, wants to know his origin. In the first state, perhaps the occurrence of the first experience of *An*, he turns to such natural phenomena as the sun, moon, sea and stars for an answer. After some time (actually further awareness) the answer proves unsatisfactory.

After a long striving, the seeker is referred to Adam who

considers himself inadequate to give the answer. Yet one feels that an *An*, a creative moment, is taking place, that is, a leap from idol worship to God, a centre of the human urge. Having not found the proper answer in Adam, the seeker goes to Moses who suggests 'patience'. Is patience and persistence essential for the manifestation of *An?* I believe so. However, the seeker is also referred to Christ, symbolizing love and affection. But still he is not totally born, for he desires further fulfilment. Then he is referred to Muhammad, symbolizing a new manifestation of '*An* in time', but Muhammad though helpful asks the seeker to search further within his own faculties; senses, reason, imagination, and heart (the synthesis of all faculties). The seeker in an *An* of exploration hears the voice of the senses admit that it is the source of diversity. The seeker is referred to reason. Reason gives considerable help to the seeker but admits that it does not have all the answers. Then in a moment of experience the seeker becomes aware of imagination. Imagination admits that it is the source of unity but also warns that its unitary efforts often tend to become illusionary. The seeker now turns to 'heart' as the real means of acquiring unitary experience. The heart accepts the seeker but also tells him that it can only motivate him; he must find union with the object of desire only through his own efforts.[15]

This process of inner search and inner evolution of man as described by one of the great enlightened men of all ages, 'Attar, discloses the invisible factors active day and night in order to prepare humans and non-humans for the experience of *An*. The history of the development of Persian religious thought is another illustration of the manifestation of *An*. At the beginning, the worship of natural phenomena, magic and sacrificial duties provided an answer to man's search for meaning. Then it became imitative theist, and formalistic religion. Later the culture developed and at last the rationalist transcended the imitative faith, deism manifested itself, and finally with the failure of intellectualism in the eleventh and twelfth centuries, the experiential process, the Sufi way of birth and rebirth, became the fulfilment of the seeker.[16] Thus there are indications that the history of inner evolution of man is the real answer to man's fulfilment and such a history is rich with experiences of *An*. In fact, man has had no other way to transcend his inner core than through an experience of *An*, or experience of original moments.

What we also learn from the experience of *An* as a mechanism of inner evolution, so beautifully told by 'Attar in the allegorical tongue of heart, is that heart must motivate, and the seeker must search for the star (the object of desire). When the star hits the heart, and the heart reaches for the star – then out of such a unity an *An* is born.

Hierarchy in the experience of *An*

The Sufis believed in multi-reality. In the study of *Final Integration in the Adult Personality*,[17] I have further added that all integrated men of the East and West have discovered the existence of multi-realities, basically natural, cultural, historical and existential. To the Sufis, the validity of the existence of multiple realities was based on the principle that each reality possesses its own language, its own values, and its own symbols; and furthermore, each is ruled by its own general law of detachment and unification. At each state the seeker must identify himself with the object of desire through experience of *An*. This psychological law is instrumental both within the sphere of a single reality and as a means of birth passing from one sphere of reality to another. Known Sufis who contributed to this principle in its conceptualization were Abu-al Futuh al-Suhrawardi,[18] Abu-al Sharif al Barwili al Shadhili,[19] A. al-Gillani,[20] and Nur-al-din Jami.[21]

I have specifically mentioned these few great Sufis because they represented a special sect of Sufism, which believed in esoteric illumination. Real knowledge was viewed as coming out of the experience of *An* – instant illumination. They even characterized man *par excellence* as one who can have true knowledge through *ishragh* (illumination in an *An*). All these

Sufis defined *An* as absolute simplicity, resulting from union; this experience was also referred to as a moment of manifestation (*al-tajalli*) or moment of union (*al-jama*). A hierarchy of illumination was also present in their thinking. The lowest category represented the illumination of name, where name symbolized conceptual reality. At the next level was the illumination of attributes. (Here one recalls Berkeley's argument that an object is an aggregate of qualities, but the one difference is that Berkeley utilized the power of intellect in his argument whereas the Sufis came to recognize the state as they were experiencing it.) The third stage was the illumination of essence. To illustrate these stages the Sufis used metaphors, for example, 'one cannot pluck a rose out of R-O-S-E', that is, one can perceive diversity and form (name) but unity is in essence. Similarly, grapes are countable, but if they are crushed they become one. In modern semantics Bertrand Russell speaks of 'classes of nouns', and modern physics has given us an extensive gradation of colour. In all ages literary men, and more recently, psychologists have written, in general terms, of the intensity of emotion, although an index of such an intensity is not available. Therefore in all degrees of illumination, hierarchies exist.[22]

In brief then, to arrive at the experience of *An* three illuminating techniques with their innumerable possibilities are necessary: (1) the illumination of names, (2) illumination of attributes and (3) illumination of essence; the sequence is the reverse of childhood experience. If such experiences occur, they recreate our original nature and give insight into humanity. Through the process of illumination of name one discovers history, one's own mental history and beyond that, one arrives at the state of objects with certain qualities. One is no longer aware of words in their abstract form, but the constant relatedness to the original object which produced the word. Through the illumination of qualities one arrives at waves, light, and the original elements of the object, which are the sources of shape, colour and sound. These two techniques have already been experienced by original physicists, and are taught by second-level physicists.

It is the illumination of essence which proves difficult to explain and occurs only to a highly sensitive psyche. There is evidence that only a few so-called miracle workers such as Abu Said Ibn Abi 'l-Khayr, al-Hallaj, Rumi, Moses, Christ and Muhammad attained such a state. In explaining the highest state of the Master Sufi, al-Ghazzali noted that Sufis were not only able to move their own bodies but also human and non-human bodies around them.[23] The possibility of such a great breakthrough, though now out of the reach of man, can give man hope of uncovering both the original motive of the universe in physics and the structure of the genes in biology.

The process of the manifestation of *An*

The process which produces a unitary experience, that is, an *An* of life, is no doubt the I-thou relationship. 'Thou' can be any object of desire, and 'I' can be any person at any stage who is incited by the proper object of desire. In the process of union of 'I' and 'thou' the essential is the inner motivation of the seeker. The heart must be motivated from within. The thou, the object of desire, must be worthy enough. In Sufi literature the purity of heart, the most essential of all, and the intention are often compared to a clear mirror. If one's mirror, through socialization, competition, marriage, and professional recognition, has become dulled, then the seeker needs more cleansing than even an illiterate but natural man.

In any case, when the seeker chooses the path, he notices his object of desire, and the bent is total concentration for union with the object of desire. This intensive effort is expressed in terms of the lover-beloved relationship; including a process by which the total effort of the seeker is directed towards bringing the lover to the state of *ghorb* (closeness). Therefore it is necessary initially that one also becomes aware of the pitfalls along the way. The most serious pitfall of the I-thou relationship is when the 'I', knowingly and unknowingly, enters the process of union in order to obtain the object of desire for himself (the lover) rather than for its own sake. The requirement is sincerity and further sincerity. To be certain of their sincerity the Sufis followed signs and symbols; they watched over the rise and fall of their desires, and in addition analysed the motives of such desires, and then adopted various exercises including spiritual dances.

When I becomes 'thou', duality turns into unity, resulting in an *An* – a new state, new feeling, and a situation in which one becomes aware of his previous states and can communicate symbolically, holistically and through experiential media. The psychological laws of the I-thou relationship which yield to unitary experience involve basically three elements: the 'I', known in Sufism as lover; 'thou' or the beloved; and the process, known as 'love'. At the end of experience these three elements are supposed to become one. The expression 'knower', 'knowing', and 'known' are also used, but knowledge here does not refer to intellectual knowledge but to the intuitive aspect. Subject and object and process have also been used as terms. One of the earliest Sufi mystics who developed this system was Shaikh Abu al Futuh Maj-dal-din Ahmad Ibn Muhammad Ghazzali Tusi, whose eldest brother after having gained fame in philosophy and theology accepted his point of view and became a transcendentalist.

Ahmad Ghazzali wrote the *Treatise on Love* for an anonymous friend whom he called 'dearer than brother' and who requested his work. In this small forty-page treatise, Ahmad Ghazzali views love as a phenomenon having no dimension; he further relates that just as eyes are for seeing and ears for hearing, the heart is the instrument of love, and if one does not utilize it, the loss is like not using one's eyes and brain. Therefore, this universal organ has a specific purpose and can be utilized by any man at any stage of evolution. A heart without an object of desire is a man without a goal and restless. As soon as he falls in love, he finds himself in a state of 'intimacy' and an acceptance of the world – two basic prerequisites of man's healthy function. The nature of 'love', according to Ahmad

Ghazzali, is beyond the limitation of thinking and ordinary science. In order to convey this point he mentions that through ordinary science we can reach the shore, but 'love' is diving into the ocean. Then our ordinary consciousness is of no assistance.

At the beginning the lover is like static energy until, at the proper time, the proper object of desire attracts him. Then his static energy turns into a dynamic force. The direction of this dynamic force is always toward 'Thou' the beloved. Just as the traveller on a sea voyage always watches the North Star, so too the lover always looks towards the beloved, regardless of the direction in which he is being led. At the beginning the beloved is the strength of the lover, whereas at the end the lover becomes the beloved's strength. However, this process is not so simple. Ghazzali tells us that in the first stage when the lover begins to seek the beloved there is a period of denial of love. The lover denies that he is in love and the beloved is changing his ideas, and like the sun on a cloudy day appears and disappears. This early stage may lead to conflict between the lovers, and it may also produce guilt in the lovers arising from their deviation from public and conventional opinion. In order to transcend such guilt, the Sufis often took bold steps and encountered reality by actualizing new but unpopular reality. (Perhaps some of today's youth apply this process with or without knowing its therapeutic aspect.) To overcome great pride resulting from wealth and power, a Master Sufi of the ninth century sent Shebli, the novice Sufi and a governor's son to knock at every door, introduce himself and beg for daily bread until he had emptied himself of the pompousness of his social status.

Now assuming that one has transcended the early obstacles arising from the I-thou relationship, and one has fallen in the path of love, not out of need but out of a genuine urge, then the course of true love and the path toward union with the object of desire starts. At this stage the beloved is the strength of the lover. The beloved's friends are the lover's friends and her enemies his enemies, but as the intensity of the love grows, the relationship changes. The lover does not like his beloved's associates even to look at her. He becomes jealous – or in the apt words of Ghazzali, he wants intimacy, that is, separation from the others and a move toward him. As the intense love strengthens its roots in the heart of the lover, he even considers his being for the beloved. He is totally committed, devoted, and is constantly seeking her satisfaction. He seeks her in human and non-human objects. The story is told of Majnum (the Romeo of the East) who saved an antelope from a hunter; when the hunter asked him why he did it, he replied that the antelope's eyes reminded him of the eyes of Lila (Juliet of the East). Similarly, one can observe himself. When we are intensely involved with someone we may see her in other faces erroneously. Here I am not referring to an error of the senses, but to the power of the beloved's image on the lover. In the process of the growth of love, Ghazzali talks of symbols which can be helpful, both external signs and gestures arising from the beauty of the beloved and invisible signs manifested from experience and communications which have passed between the beloved and the lover.

If this true love continues, the love eventually becomes the mirror of the beloved. He notices her in himself. He has in the process become empty and fills himself with her qualities. He has freed himself of every idol and related totally to his object of desire. The strength of the lover increases until he realizes the beauty and potentiality of the beloved better than himself. (Perhaps it is because of this reality of lover that even in the ordinary sense the beauty and qualities of one's partner becomes more important to the male partner than to the female.) Finally, the lover feels the real 'self' of the beloved even better than she until he believes that he is the beloved herself. There is no longer duality; unity prevails. This one becomes that one. It is at this stage that *An* is experienced, but only after: (1) removal of guilt; (2) removal of self-deception, and (3) removal of public opinion. It is the gradual experiencing of the beloved in the moment of *Itasal* (union) and in the moment of *Fragh* (separation), in presence, in absence, in daytime and in dreams wherein suddenly the *An* takes hold of both, and in that instant *An* appears as thunder, as a flash of light, as love itself. No longer is there lover or beloved, or more precisely all three elements have become one force. In my work on final integration, I have expressed the view that superego, ego, and id (if indeed such a division exists in healthy people) finally becomes one creative victor. The result of this union gradually appears in the life of the participants. For instance, a change of psyche takes place when initially the beloved is the source of strength of the lover; now the lover becomes the source of transcendental strength of the beloved.

The process of identification between I and thou indicates the process of motivation and integration in man, a concept most fully developed by the afore-mentioned Farid al Din 'Attar. The process of identification constitutes the essence of 'Attar's teaching. Through the process of search 'I' becomes 'thou'. This union has been most aptly described by 'Attar in his allegory, *The Conference of the Birds*:[24]

> *And if they looked at both together, both were*
> *the Simurgh, neither more nor less.*
> *This one was that, and that one this; the like*
> *of this hath no one heard in the world.*

In this allegory the object of search is God, although two centuries before 'Attar, al-Hallaj (Mansur) after his transformation explicitly claimed, 'Ana 'l-Hagh' ('I am the creative truth – God'). Though aware that he would be crucified for his ideas, al-Hallaj considered his union with the perfect image of God a natural process of human inner evolution. Like all other Sufis he perceived man as a potential being who, through intense love for his object of desire, can transform himself. Furthermore, he considered this union, *hulul*, the true way of worship:[25]

> *Thy spirit is mingled in my spirit, even*
> *as wine is mingled with pure water.*
> *When anything touches thee, it touches me too,*
> *In every case, Thou art I.*

Later, Rumi gave a more precise interpretation of the Union and considered Hallaj's claim (Ana 'l-Hagh) as a genuine expression of humility toward God (object of desire), for in this way one eliminated the duality of the existence between oneself and the object of desire. Rumi pointed out that in this claim the lover has lost self-existence; he is the beloved, whereas in the common claim, 'I am God's slave', the individual is still in the state of dual existence between himself and God.

One of the earliest Persian Sufis, Abu Yazid, expressed this union of I–thou in a short phrase: 'For thirty years God was my mirror, now I am my own mirror.'[26] This union of I–thou has also been described as 'transforming union', as *ittahad*, *itasal*, identification, deification and spiritual marriage. In brief, it has been viewed as de-embedding oneself, emptying oneself (*fana*) in order to embed oneself in life, immortality and totality. Rumi maintained that in 'love' there is no room for 'we' and 'I'. He also perceived his experience of *An* as a trip without 'we', intoxication without wine, remembrance without 'we', and happiness without 'we'.[27]

However, it makes little difference by whatever name and metaphor the process of the union of I–thou was called. What is important is that this process required an intensive experience of concentration, first on one's self so that one could purify onself of unsuitable past experiences; second, on his object of desire in such a way that every human and non-human sign would bring him to their presence. This experience required at times that the group chant the name of the object of desire (God, Allah) so that the group would notice nothing except Him. It was customary for certain Sufi dances to begin with *zikr*, the exaltation of Allah. I also believe that this chanting, accompanied by circular motions, regulated the Sufis' breathing, stimulated their organism and reduced their conscious power.

To today's reader, such an aim may appear as suitable only to a small select group, the Sufis. What about the ordinary man? Actually, Sufis differed from others (both intellectuals and ordinary people) only in their goal and object of desire.

A great Sufi, Ibn al Arabi, explained the matter thus:[28]

> *Love, qua love, is one and the same reality to those*
> *Arab lovers and to me, but the objects of our love*
> *are different, for they love a phenomenon, whereas*
> *I love the real.*

Thus, the process of the I–thou relationship is a mechanism of awareness and enlightenment and a way to develop insight into life. It can happen at any level. I personally believe that this is the mechanism with which children begin; it is the process by which one identifies with one's parents, one's cultural representatives, with one's professional ideals, and it is especially the means of union between intimate partners. In my recent studies of creativity, I have indicated that this very process is the common denominator which all innovators have adopted. The originators have always arrived at their inventions through this mechanism, although sometimes after an intensive mental exercise.[29] There is much evidence in Persian culture to show that scholars, scientists, sincere religious leaders, literary men, artists, craftsmen, teachers, and even statesmen discovered that the experience of *An* is the ultimate source of meaningfulness and life expression. What Albert Schweitzer referred to as 'mysticism' – the transcendence state of all mental endeavour – perhaps also manifests itself in the highest form of *An* experience. In the process of growth I shall cite some Persian thinkers who having reached the zenith of their field of endeavour found themselves dissatisfied until they eventually adopted an experiental approach to life and arrived at a significant unitary experience.

The apex of the psyche is the seat of creative imagination, that unique ability which is ignored by modern psychologists. Creative imagination is the vehicle for unifying man's various faculties. At the opportune moment of such a unification, one notices a new relationship, one becomes aware of a new configuration, one receives and experiences a new illumination. Now one can overlook what one has experienced, enjoy the image for its delight or long for more, or try to form it into a product until a new situation arises. One can become faithful to what he has experienced or ignore it. When the individual finds the process of formation fulfilling or appreciates its value he definitely forms it into a product. If he is a master, an able craftsman, and is equipped with the means and techniques, he will directly, without delay, actualize that creative vision and attain a 'higher consciousness', including an inner satisfaction and enrichment of the cultural product or human relatedness. However, if he exists in a dual state of mind and he experiences these creative flashes only occasionally, he has no choice but to hand it over to the power of practical imagination – to the active mind – to the realm of thinking which will measure it, evaluate it from the utilitarian point of view and question its validity and truthfulness until the mind accepts or rejects it. If this vision is rejected (which is definitely due to a barrier within the ego) for further growth, it is left in the dark mist with all other forgotten ideas for others, perhaps more sensitive persons, to discover. However, if its utilitarian aspect becomes apparent the mind may try to give it form. If such a rational or scientific person has the means, techniques and favourable social atmosphere, he may, with some effort, produce a new tool or product. However, if he has no proper technique, lacks means, or has to work within a conflict-ridden situation, he will face innumerable frustrations. He may get so involved with the conflict within and outside himself, that he may forsake his original idea. Even if he succeeds in his long fight for success, he may eventually become successful but without inner fulfilment and without inner satisfaction. In every age this has been the significant difference between the fragmented man in search of success outside himself and the totally integrative man. In essence, the difference is whether to act for the sake of fulfilment of the act, or to act for a product. In the latter case the product matters most of all, man least, in the former case selfhood is all, the product least.

Application of *An* to creativity, child-rearing, education and psychotherapy

In brief, we can now claim that *An* is the moment of conception, the instant of birth and rebirth, and the experience of joy and originality. Its mechanism of growth is a dynamic relation between subject and object where initially the subject depends on the object of desire, in the second place there is an instant of union, followed by the object's dependence on the subject, and finally, the state where each experiences union independently within the universe.

In this sense the nature and process of *An* is similar to human creativity, where a long period of mental effort, tension, patience and struggle within the group precedes a relaxed state in which the individual innovates and creates something new. Such an original production in art, science, religion, or politics or whatever is only possible if the creator first perceives the vision, becomes faithful to it, notices its distance from his own reality and then, even in spite of adverse public opinion, makes an effort to materialize it through unification with it.

I personally believe that this is the true nature of man. The real state of the uncontaminated child before socialization and primitive man before civilization is based on such a psychological make-up. In other words, both in the child and in primitive man, the 'creative image', the means of experiencing *An*, existed before 'thinking' became the instrument of reason and judgment. *An* existed before concept was born. However, the course of human history has kept man from retaining this pure quality. Thus each of us is born, and only by assimilating the group's accumulated cultural experience and later leaving it, is it possible to become creative and to experience *An* again. What is needed is a new atmosphere for child-rearing and education based on reality, and the continuity of *An* organically develops first. This new type of child-rearing should emphasize the experiential quality of human communication and recognize that the human child is a unity capable of experiencing

An. By completely accepting these principles we will act differently in child-rearing and early education.

I consider the application of the concept of *An* to child-rearing and education a direct path; it is a unitary and experiential path based on the following steps:

(1) No child will be helped to conceptualize and enter the world of 'name' without the experience of such a name and concept.

(2) No child should enter of the world of 'name' and concept without having received his 'experience' – however simple it is – and without having given it some sort of form.

(3) Reading, writing, and arithmetic should only be taught through the creation of those forms the child has discovered and given a name.

(4) Socialization must take place through identification rather than through verbalization. In fact, at the age of about 2 to 3, children naturally identify with all types of professional persons – postmen, cashiers, typists, doctors, librarians – those with whom they come in contact. Moreover, it is important that this real face-to-face experience gradually replaces television and other mass media. This human experience is necessary and valuable.

(5) School and society must be an extension of the home. Therefore, teachers and parents must be re-educated to accept these assumptions. Only by application of the principle of *An* experienced harmoniously at home, school, and in social interactions with children is it possible to preserve the original unity so essential for the further experience of *An*.

(6) The assimilation of culture is necessary if each generation is to experience a deeper layer of *An*: at the same time if this assimilation is done on the basis of time schedules (as is true of present school curricula) and if it is geared to subject matter, then the original unity will be split and delegated to the realm of 'thinking' and rote learning. Yet a unitary teacher with insight into the real structure of culture and psyche can avoid this split. How?

Continuance of the original unitary state of the child during the period of assimilation of culture is possible as long as the child is interested in one subject such as reading. He should be left alone to pursue the subject related to his real experience. If he is satiated, the child will request an opportunity for new experience. I see no harm in a child continuing this one subject matter to the point of mastery. After all, all subjects taught in school can be related, in one way or another, to 'language' or to mathematics.

(7) Such learning must take place slowly and accurately, not for the sake of speed, but to enhance discovery. For instance, at the age of three and a half, my daughter became interested in reading and writing due to a favourable home environment. I then gave her a pencil and a small note book and asked her to sit next to me at the table and write whatever she wanted. In a few minutes she had covered a whole page with all types of scribbles. I went over the page with her, and those which looked like English letters I named for her. In a few days of such practice she learned the alphabet, and she continued to identify letters on outside signs and on printed pages. The same process was followed for the discovery of letter sounds and numbers. This principle can be applied in many fields.

(8) In the higher states of assimilation, as soon as the child can read, biographies and autobiographies of people who have had real experiences should be emphasized. At the age of eight and a half, my son had read over fifty such works, and through the discovery of the life of real people, he had also discovered the geography of earth, nature, minerals, and various aspects of the natural and behavioural sciences.

(9) Later on, an opportunity must be provided for the actual experimentation of original scientists with emphasis on what the young child's inclinations demand, until he finds the one person, whether past or present with whom he can identify. Such an identification provides the foundation for a useful profession and basis of birth into unity. All these nine points can be achieved before the age of adolescence.

(10) As adolescence dawns, emphasis should be given to: (a) the discovery of social institutions and current events,

(b) discovery of history, and above all, (c) discovery of the opposite sex, (d) intimate relationships, (e) discovery of love as a natural mechanism of the experience of union, (f) application to other discoveries of human destiny, (g) perception of the process of experiencing *An* through intimate relations with one's own partner, and (h) continuity of human creativity and man's unfolding through the process of rearing children.

If such steps are followed at home, school, and in social institutions, the original totality is nourished, and the natural creative imagination will enrich itself resulting in fulfilment. However, social pathology, resulting from an historical orientation, uncreative parents, unimaginative teachers and immature leaders have thwarted this process. Consequently, by the age of six or seven the child loses his state of totality, his spontaneity diminishes. Ill-education accompanied by the consequences of social institutions have stymied man's original nature and left him a fragmented person, and perhaps ultimately mentally ill and in need of psychotherapy. Thus, the question arises; what is the contribution of a 'philosophy' of *An* to psychotherapy?

The greatest contribution of the art of the *An* experience is in terms of the master–disciple relationship, specifically, the master's total commitment to 'care' and the disciple's devotion. This relationship based on human worth is only possible if one has an intense 'creative passion' for turning a potential fragmented man into a whole one. In my opinion, no fee can bring about such a relationship, and it is still more difficult if it is done on an hourly basis. The majority of Freudian-derived concepts are inadequate, culture-bound and reflect certain commercial values created by the marketing orientation of the late nineteenth and early twentieth centuries. Of course, there are exceptions, but many psychiatrist-technicians have become disheartened and have failed in their service to their fellow men because they have taken the responsibility of helping another human being solely in exchange for a fee. Indeed, detrimental social conditions today reflect in part the consequences of other professional duties – legislative, legal, educational – if done on a purely monetary basis, they do not give fruitful results.

A further contribution of the philosophy of *An* to Western psychotherapy deals with the real assumption of human nature as an entity. Thus any therapy must emphasize conditions which will contribute to the restoration of a unitary experience and result in a spontaneous cure. For instance, a pre-verbal child in the care of a mother who cannot understand his non-verbal signs becomes irritable and perhaps neurotic, but as soon as he learns to speak, a spontaneous cure is possible, and it would appear that many neurotic symptoms disappear. However, this judgment is based on only a few cases of mothers of children between the ages of ten months and twenty-two months.

Consequently, we can conclude that with the acceptance of the principle of *An*, therapy as a technique takes on a new form. It is seen as a continual experiential exchange between therapist and patient until the situation is ripe for the spontaneous experience of cure. In such a relationship both therapist and patient are active, the major difference being that the therapist notices the succession of signs, interprets them and enlightens the course of events of the patient, whereas the patient remains unaware of this situation. On the basis of this assumption, the *An* experience and spontaneous therapy derived from it contradict several traditional Freudian analytical approaches: it makes a passive analyst active, it encourages a patient to become expressive rather than talkative, it transcends the symptom-cure and leads the analyst toward experience and an understanding of the origin of the attitude of the real measure for developing a healthy character. Rather than make the patient self-conscious and aware of the negative aspect of the unconsciousness, the therapist will direct him to new original experiences whose accumulative present expands to a new state, a new disintegration or a new integration, a new separation or relatedness directed toward a decrease of past tradition, good and bad, and the rise of naturalness, sensitivity, receptivity, understanding, and the utilitarian service of thought, reason and concept, and differentiating this quality from the prevailing dominant role of impulse and ego in modern man.

Furthermore, according to the experiential philosophy of *An*, no cure can result from becoming conscious of the neurosis of our time. In fact, it is a hindrance to man. In order to regain our original unitary status, we must either create a new force which can encounter and defeat the childhood and social experiences and create a synthesis, or assist us to forget and if possible, erase it entirely from our psyche, rather than to become aware of it. In fact, the division of the psyche in terms of id, ego, and superego deviates from the experiential psychotherapy of *An*. Actually, what is essential is our 'totality' on the one hand, and real experience on the other. The therapist-patient relationship must follow a design (each according to his situation) so that these two qualities become active again. According to my system of thought the direct path to the re-establishment of such a relationship offers the greatest benefit through various non-verbal mechanisms, such as creative experience, songs, music, writing, crafts, art, and relating these products to the emotional experience of the patient by the therapist in a way that the chain of events creates a new experience of awareness for the patient and leads to a deeper realization of man as a totality. The Sufis were activists and their minds always developed new symbols. They advise us that the best remedy for a restless mind is to concentrate on physical activity for regaining bodily grace, and when the body is restless, we must emphasize meditation. In other words, the control of the response to the demand of the psyche or the body is essential for cure.

Finally, the Sufis would accept the idea of transference in modern psychotherapy, but not as a projection of the parent–child relationship; rather they perceive it as a holistic approach for the identification with a realistic state of the master in order for the seeker to receive the grace and blessing of the next state. In this sense the experiential therapy of *An* is forward looking rather than stressing the past relations. In this light, Ernest G. Schachtel's meaningful essay on amnesia in childhood[30] deserves further interpretation. Indeed the role of amnesia is of great importance in experiential therapy; great Eastern sages have often failed to record their childhood because they consider it unimportant to them; to them the significance concerns the *end*, the beloved, and this should be seen in the mirror of the being so that one's own motive and effort match the goal.

Summary

The Sufi concept *An* emphasizes a crucial moment; it requires the total involvement of the individual, it depends upon visible but primarily invisible human and non-human forces, and expresses an existential, living and creative moment of life at its fullest. Furthermore, it is related to a 'cosmic harmony', or more precisely, the harmonization of man with cosmic rhythm; and is the climax of cumulative events and a succession of invisible happenings – attainable only by receptive persons who follow the proper signs and symbols.

In other words, *An* is the moment of conception, birth and rebirth, the instant of 'noticing' and the moment of creation and creativity. It is the climax of love, of deep communication and the spark of life. The nature of such a spark of life, *An*, is intensive and is therefore non-transferable; it is spaceless, thus immeasureable by our ordinary senses and logic. It requires purity and sincerity, truthfulness and one's own capacities. It is essentially a matter of deep expressive feeling – non-temporal and beyond discursive intellect. It appears as a 'pregnant' idea after the individual has experienced it and become aware of it. It is creation and re-creation requiring purity of attitude, total concentration and the baring of sensitivity to sense perceptions, memories and associations, that is, to all elements which have no bearing on the present, the moment.

The experience of *An* is not of the nature of casuality. It does not share any quality with the material structure of the world.

It is not even related to the world of attributes, but it is the manifestation of the world of essence, meaning the original notion of action. Thus, it is the essence in the crystallization of the world of 'name', and 'attributes' which one must seek illumination.

The appearance of *An*, the moment of creative vision, is also the moment of union with one's object of desire. In the process of being, in the process of rebirth the object of desire is the guide, but in the first state the seeker, *Ibn al vaght* (the son of 'time') becomes the Sufi *Abu al vaght* (the father of 'time') that is, the instant of the experience of *An*. In a sense, *An* is also the experience of union, and it is also the moment of intense joy and happiness: this feeling is the result of the I-thou union and is so strong that if one has experienced it in any sphere of life, one longs for its recurrence and makes great preparation for the re-experience of the moment. Those who failed have sometimes turned to hashish (but they only became imitators). Those who kept to their original naturalness, even though illiterate, experienced it, and those who had emotional, intellectual and cultural blocks had to struggle with inner and outer conflicts until they reharmonized themselves – the beginning of preparation for the occurrence of the *An* experience.

The experience of *An* is the crown of the transcendental psychology of Persian culture, and intellectuals, poets, religious leaders, philosophers and scientists who assimilated the culture of their times finally found shelter under this protective umbrella which gave them time to relate their knowledge to the experiential root and revitalize themselves. Indeed, an analytical study of these soul-searching Persians would make a significant contribution to the contemporary existential search for rebirth in totality.

Islamic and pre-Islamic Persian scholars in all fields of thought whether theologians, philosophers, scientists, mathematicians or astronomers, ultimately arrived at cosmology and the search for meaning, culminating in the concept of *An*, best represented in the school of Sufism – the art of rebirth and experiential living.

I have further indicated that this experiential moment is not rare. More people exprience it than scholars are aware. Our original unitary state is full of it, but due to erroneous child-rearing and education we alienate ourselves from its occurrence and we become fragmented individuals requiring psychotherapy. Yet the history of modern psychotherapy is gradually entering the era of psycho-cultural analysis which will lead to experiential therapy; in that stage the experience of *An* will provide us with the necessary theory and practice.

Chapter 9
Conclusion

The Sufis were a group of searching men who discovered the realities of human experience by realizing that we are all under-developed. One must view oneself in the perspective of evolution and change, that is, in order to know one's 'true self'. Just as we progressively evolved from the inorganic to the animal state, and to our present social state, so too can we further evolve from this state of social being to the cosmic state.

Once awakened, the individual realizes that the same evolutionary process which led him to his present state is continually at work. This process may further develop his mind, and make him realize his need as a religious or an intellectual man. At the next stage he becomes familiar with the idols in his mind and attempts to break them all in order to achieve his new state of life. At this point the Sufi advances to a level of being as far above the ordinary man as that of man in relation to his earlier existence. The fully-awakened one attains union with all and helps his cosmic self come to light. He becomes a universal man remembering the entire past in the sense of evolution and seeing the whole of life in even a small particle.

Having had an image of such a better life, the awakened person becomes a seeker and values this image above all else. Motivated by it, he longs for it, becomes concerned with it and directs his efforts toward attaining it so as to become one with it. He becomes competitive, but only with himself, for competition with one's self constitutes perfection.

Man's nature, however, does not easily bend toward perfection. While his insight may make him aware of a better life, his instincts, drives and selfish motives, or *nafs*, as the Sufis refer to them, may pull him down. Caught by contradictory forces in his nature, he becomes anxious. If he is lucky he stands at the threshold of two worlds: his ego stands up against his potential or real self; the universal man against the social. In modern times people generally do not recognize this disharmony within themselves. When uneasy, they take a pill, a drink or escape to an illusory way of life. They achieve tranquillity only as they can ignore their situation. However, if an individual, like the Sufi novice, analyses his situation and becomes critical of it he cannot exchange his ultimate certainty for temporary satisfaction. He becomes even more concerned with his existential problem. As a searcher of the truth he recognizes *that he has only one heart and is potentially one entity; he cannot split into several parts.* Recognizing that only the truth can save him, he concentrates solely on union, where union means identification with the desired object and disunion the heart's attachment to several objects. The object of this search consists in the realization of the real self, the state of perfect (universal) man, unity with all, becoming God-like or being only the truth. To become like God means the assimilation of what God represents, that is, a beautiful creation rather than submission to the image of God; *loving to save, not loving to be saved.*

The removal of the self in reality means the annihilation of those experiences which bar the revealing of the real self. Sufis call the experience of removal of 'I' *fana*, which ends in a state of ecstasy, the feeling of union; it is the beginning of *baqa*, the state of conscious existence.

The Sufi's goal is now clear, but how can he achieve it? First of all he must understand the limitations of his consciousness, specifically, that it contains unnecessary material and that in its development numerous veils have formed around the real self preventing it from manifesting its true nature. Once he recognizes this fact the Sufi can remove the 'I' from consciousness: a state which is identical with changing and expanding consciousness to function in harmony with the unconscious.

As a first step in this direction the Sufi must inactivate *nafs* (the source of impulses) or more precisely, use his reason to control passion. Sufism recognizes, as does modern psychology, that this part of our being cannot be eliminated or suppressed entirely. *Nafs* also possesses a great negative power, a kind of force like anger or passionate love which blinds the intellect. Therefore, the Sufi seeks to satisfy *nafs* before bringing it under the control of intellect. Even then it will persist, just as embers glow under the ashes; nor must the seeker then ignore it, for at any time when the embers flare up, they must be quenched again. Some Sufis believe that ordinarily after the individual has satisfied *nafs*, in terms of both sex impulses and those relating to success and greed, he must then gradually restrict it and bring it under the control of reason.

Because of this factor in human nature, Sufism attracts mature individuals rather than youth. The forceful nature of *nafs* also explains why Sufis believe that ordinary men need religious experience, even if it is only partially understood. In a positive sense the Sufis control *nafs* by virtuous behaviour and righteous deeds. For instance when a seeker presents himself to a guide for the purpose of becoming a Sufi, he is put on probation for three years: the first year to serve people, the second to serve God and the third to observe the rise and fall of his own desires. The seeker disengages *nafs* from its qualities thereby directing its downward tendency towards the pursuit of his goal. In this process he becomes indifferent to material possession and eliminates passion-arousing desires. Now united in thought, action and feeling, he prepares to rid his mind of all conscious thoughts.

The Sufi purposely adopts a period of isolation in order to remove illusionary consciousness, that is, he adopts a method opposite to that of its development. For the Sufi this temporary period of isolation is the most effective method of self-analysis. He believes that society and culture are a bridge for attaining the real self. Even the lives of such great prophets as Moses, Muhammad, Buddha, of notable Sufis like Prince Abrahim Adham and Abi Sa'id Abi-Alkhayr reveal the adoption of a similar state in order to achieve the true self. Through the method of isolation the Sufi tries to rid himself of illusionary material in consciousness, which means that he has to analyse every single experience in his mind, understand its imperfections, and at the same time develop a thorough affection for it and see his relatedness to it. In this analysis the Sufi detaches himself from society, but he also develops a receptivity and appreciation of every element in our world, relating it to its original existence. He becomes unaware of what he once thought perfect or knowledge he had gained, but meanwhile his immediate experiences enrich his being by activating his insight, fostering love and developing discernment in him. Love becomes the vehicle which carries him forward. 'Love is the drug of all drugs' which strengthens his faith, removes his anxiety and encourages him to pass through numerous states of mind (ahwal).

In the process of experiencing ahwal, he undergoes a series of internal changes, or if you will, he lives a multitude of lives. Continually on guard and in love, he guards against falling into an illusion and attaching himself to its object of search. According to Sufism those who are on guard and in love find no rest. This restlessness produces energy for further contemplation and searching of every corner of the mind in order to prepare the psyche for the appearance of the real self. In this state he receives guidance to encourage the real self to make its appearance. When awake he concentrates on his object of search, when asleep he begs his real self to appear before him. The Sufi's object of love reveals itself in dreams and he must be ready to receive its call. In traditional Iran the Sufi orders strongly believed that many mysteries would be unfolded in their dreams.

In essence, the Sufi's task is to break the idol of the phenomenal self, which is the mother-idol; having achieved this aim his search ends. Empty-handed, empty-minded and desireless, he is and he is not. He has and he has not the feeling of existence. He knows nothing, he understands nothing. He is in love, but with whom he is not aware. His heart is at the same time both full and empty of love. In the process of search he removes 'I' but he remains still aware of being unconscious of consciousness.

In the next step he loses this awareness (the awareness of the absence of consciousness) in order to eliminate the subject-object relation and achieve union. In a positive sense he assimilates all the particles of love and insight that he has felt through the process of emptying his consciousness. He transcends time and place. This state of union, the climax of the annihilation of the partial self, is identical with ecstasy and gives the impression of a natural intoxication. Among the Persian Sufis this painless ecstatic trance sometimes lasted for days and weeks. It is a state of mind which can be termed unconsciously conscious and functions with perfect precision.

The individual has now experienced life first hand. He feels no distance between himself and his object of love. Sufis who have ended their search usually develop this state of union through certain recollections, dances, music and auto-hypnosis. Having tested it, they may again lose it. The mystery of deep love which flows in their lyrics like the current of the sea stems from union and disunion. In the following lines Abu Said describes this state of union:

> I am love; I am the beloved; no less am I the lover.
> I am the mirror and I am the beauty.
> Therefore behold me in myself.

A Sufi may stop at the stage of *fana*, which can be defined as passing from consciousness to the world of unconsciousness where reason is active. He may also pass beyond this stage and find himself in the state of *baqa* (continuance) where he gains individuality in non-individuality, that is, infusion has taken place but the individual has entered a state of conscious existence. Whosoever achieves this state becomes a 'perfect man', who relies on consciousness and is ruled by reason. Aided by intuition the perfect man functions as a totality, with spontaneity and expressiveness. Instead of studying life from afar he is life itself. In this state, indescribable and characterized by silence, the individual is now everything or nothing: everything in the sense that he is united with all, nothing in the sense that nothingness is the beginning of 'everythingness'. He embraces all of life, he is beyond good and bad. In a practical way he has experienced qualities embracing all of life, ordinary human existence and intellectual life; he has felt himself variously as a famous man, an ambitious one, a religious man and has passed beyond all of them, finally giving rebirth to a more comprehensive self. He feels related to all mankind, experiences a concern for all beings and tries to utilize his earlier experiences for their benefit. One can sense the same feeling in the following poem by Rumi:

> If there be any lover in the world, O Muslims, – 'tis I.
> If there be any believer, infidel, or Christian hermit – 'tis I.
> The wine-dregs, the cup-bearer, the minstrel, the harp,
>   and the music,
> The beloved, the candle, the drink and the joy of the
>   drunken – 'tis I.
> The two and seventy creeds and the sects in the world
> Do not really exist: I swear by God that every creed
>   and sect – 'tis I.
> Earth and air, water and fire, knowest thou what they are?
> Earth and air, water and fire, nay, body and soul too –
>   'tis I.
> Truth and falsehood, good and evil, ease and difficulty
>   from first to last,
> Knowledge and learning and asceticism and piety and
>   faith – 'tis I.
> The fire of Hell, be assured, with its flaming limbos,
> Yes, and paradise and the Houris – 'tis I.
> This earth and heaven with all that they hold,
> Angels, Peris, Genies and Mankind – 'tis I.

Notes

1 The organic nature of self in Sufism

1 From Sir M. Iqbal, *The Reconstruction of Religious Thought in Islam*, Lahore, Ashraf Press, 1962, p. 187.

2 The structure and anatomy of conventional self

1 A. R. Arasteh, *Rumi the Persian, the Sufi*, London, Routledge & Kegan Paul, 1974, pp. 97-8.
2 Al-Ghazzali, *The Alchemy of Happiness*, trans. C. Field, Lahore, Ashraf Press, n.d., p. 14.

3 Religion: a transitional mechanism of growth to selfhood

1 Sir M. Iqbal, *The Reconstruction of Religious Thought in Islam*, Lahore, Ashraf Press, 1962, p. 85.
2 Ibid., p. 90.
3 Ibid., p. 92.

4 From being a Muslim to becoming Allah

1 Farid ud-Din Attar, *The Conference of the Birds*, trans. C. S. Nott, London, Routledge & Kegan Paul, 1967, p. 4.
2 E. G. Browne, *A Literary History of Persia*, Cambridge University Press, 1928, vol. II, p. 121.
3 Al-Ghazzali, 'Deliverance from Ignorance', quoted in M. Farzun, *The Tale of the Reed Pipe*, New York, Dutton, 1974, pp. 51-2.
4 A. Huxley, 'Visionary Experiences', in *Proceedings of the 14th International Congress of Applied Psychology*, IV, Clinical Psychology, Copenhagen, Munksgaard, 1962.

5 The rise of the inner voice and the moment of resolution

1 Al-Ghazzali, *The Confession of Al-Ghazzali*, trans. Claude Field, Lahore, Ashraf Press, n.d., p. 11.
2 Ibid., pp. 50-1.
3 Ibid., pp. 54-5.
4 A. R. Arasteh, *Rumi the Persian, the Sufi*, London, Routledge & Kegan Paul, 1974, p. 34.

6 The dual mechanism of the Sufi path

1 My father's call to prayer.
2 Farid al-Din Attar, *Muslim Saints and Mystics (Tadhkirat al-Auliya)*, trans. A. J. Arberry, London, Routledge & Kegan Paul, 1966, pp. 109-10.
3 Jalalud Din Rumi, *Teachings of Rumi: Masnavi*, ed. E. H. Whinfield, London, Octagon Press, 1974. See also A. R. Arasteh, *Rumi the Persian, the Sufi*, London, Routledge & Kegan Paul, 1974, pp. 78-9.
4 E. W. Lane, *Manners and Customs of the Modern Egyptians*, London, Dent, 1876, pp. 437-8.
5 Farid al-Din Attar, *Muslim Saints and Mystics*, pp. 105-8.
6 Jalal-ud-Din Rumi, *Mathnawi*, trans. R. A. Nicholson, vol. IV, London, Luzac, 1930, p. 381. See also A. R. Arasteh, *Final Integration in the Adult Personality*, Leiden, E. J. Brill, 1964, pp. 126-7.

7 The hierarchy of Sufi personality

1 R. A. Nicholson, *The Mystics of Islam*, London, Routledge & Kegan Paul, 1963, p. 55.
2 Ibid., p. 57.
3 Ibid.
4 New York, AMS Press, 1909, p. 197.
5 A. R. Arasteh, *Rumi the Persian, the Sufi*, London, Routledge & Kegan Paul, 1974, pp. 63-4.
6 E. G. Browne, *A Literary History of Persia*, Cambridge University Press, 1928.
7 Nicholson, *The Mystics of Islam*, p. 151.
8 Ibid.
9 Ibid., p. 160.
10 Arasteh, *Rumi the Persian, the Sufi*, p. 20.

11 K. A. Hakimi, *The Metaphysics of Rumi*, Lahore, Ashraf Press, 1959, p. 57.
12 Jalalud Din Rumi, *Diwan e Shams*, Tehran, Amir Kabir Press, 1972 (author's translation).
13 Nicholson, *The Mystics of Islam*, pp. 122–3.
14 International Congress of Psychologists, *Proceedings of the 1972 Congress*, closing session, 'Implications of Asian Psychology', Akishige, pp. 78–9.

8 *An;* creative moment: the climax of Sufi being
1 The Sufis were Muslims who transcended formalistic religion. Their doctrine has been called the art of rebirth. See A. R. Arasteh, *Man and Society in Iran*, Leiden, E. J. Brill, 1964, and *Rumi the Persian, the Sufi*, London, Routledge & Kegan Paul, 1974.
2 Arasteh, *Rumi the Persian, the Sufi*.
3 A. R. Arasteh, *Creativity in Human Development*, Cambridge, Mass., Schenkman, 1976.
4 Jalal-ud-Din Rumi, *Mathnawi*, trans. R. A. Nicholson, vol. II, London, Luzac, 1930.
5 Sir M. Iqbal, *The Reconstruction of Religious Thought in Islam*, Lahore, Ashraf Press, 1962, pp. 40–1.
6 C. Rogers, *On Becoming a Person*, Madison, University of Wisconsin Press, 1961.
7 Arasteh, *Creativity in Human Development*.
8 A. R. Arasteh, *Final Integration in the Adult Personality*, Leiden, E. J. Brill, 1964.
9 Al-Ghazzali, *The Confession of Al-Ghazzali*, trans. Claude Field, Lahore, Ashraf Press, no date, pp. 54–5.
10 Rumi, *Mathnawi*, vol. I.
11 H. Corbin and P. Kraus, 'Suhrawardi I' Aler', *Journal Asiatique*, vol. CCXXVII, Paris, 1935.
12 S. M. Afnan, *Avicenna, His Life and Works*, London, Allen & Unwin, 1958.
13 O. Khayyam, *Rubbayyat*, ed. M. Fo:ughi and M. Ghani, Tehran, Ministry of Education, 1941.
14 Jalal-ud-Din Rumi, *Fini ma Fihi (Discourses)*, ed. Fruzanfar, University of Tehran Press, 1959.
15 Farid ud-Din 'Attar, *Musibat Nama*, University of Tehran Press, 1961.

16 A. R. Arasteh, 'The development of Persian religious thought: a psychological interpretation', a series of lectures given at the University of Texas, Austin, 1964 (unpublished).

17 Arasteh, *Final Integration in the Adult Personality.*

18 A Persian executed in Aleppo in 1191. Author of *Kitab al Ishraq* (*Book of Illuministic Wisdom*), completed in 1186, *Hayaikil al Nur* (*Temples of Light*), and other works.

19 Died 1477, author of *Treatise on the Articles of Maxisms of Illumination Addressed to All Sufis* (*Mystics*), and other works.

20 Al-Gillani, author of *Al Insan al Kemel Fi Ma'rifat al Awakher Ma'l awail* (*The Perfect Man in Knowledge of Origin and End of Things*), summarized in *Studies in Islamic Mysticism* by R. Nicholson, Cambridge University Press, 1921.

21 A sixteenth-century poet-philosopher, author of *Lawa'ih* (*Flashes of Light*).

22 Relevant here are some simple observations on my own children. At the ages of 16–20 months, upon hearing songs of birds, when being asked, 'What is that?' they would reply by imitating the song of the bird. But if asked the same question a few months later, they would say, 'That's a crow,' etc. In other words, they had discovered 'name' followed by the discovery of relations, attributes, etc., a point I have elaborated further on in the last section concerning the application of *An* to psychotherapy, child-rearing and education.

23 Arasteh, *Final Integration in the Adult Personality.*

24 E. G. Browne, *A Literary History of Persia*, vols I-III, Cambridge University Press, 1928.

25 R. A. Nicholson, *The Mystics of Islam*, London, Routledge & Kegan Paul, 1963.

26 Arasteh, *Man and Society in Iran.*

27 Arasteh, *Rumi the Persian, the Sufi.*

28 Nicholson, *The Mystics of Islam*, p. 59.

29 Arasteh, *Creativity in Human Development*, p. 99.

30 E. G. Schachtel, *Metamorphosis*, New York, Basic Books, 1959.

Select bibliography

Al-Arabi, Ibn, *Tarjuman al-Ashwaq: A Collection of Mystical Odes*, trans. R. A. Nicholson, London, Luzac, 1911.

Al-Hujwiri, *Kaghf Al-Maḥjuh*, trans. R. A. Nicholson, London, Luzac, 1936.

Al Shadhili, Abu-Al Mawahib, *Qawanin Hikam Al-Ishraq* (*Illumination in Islamic Mysticism*), Princeton University Press, 1938.

Arberry, A. J., *Sufism: An account of the mystics of Islam*, London, Allen & Unwin, 1951.

Attar, Farid ud-din, *The Conference of the Birds*, London, Routledge & Kegan Paul, 1961.

'Attar, Farid ud-din, *Le Manticu 'ttair ou le langage des oiseaux*, Paris, 1864.

Browne, E. G., *A Literary History of Persia*, 4 vols, Cambridge University Press, 1928. See especially vol. III.

Iqbal, Sir M., *The secret of the self*, trans. R. A. Nicholson, London, Macmillan, 1920.

Iqbal, Sir M., *The development of metaphysics in Persia*, Lahore, Bazm-i-iqbal, 1958.

Jami, Nur ud-din Abu-ul-Rahman, *Lawa'ilm* (a treatise on Sufism), trans. E. H. Whinfield and M. M. Kazwini, London, Royal Asiatic Society, 1928.

Macdonald, D. B., *The Religious Attitude and Life in Islam*, New York, AMS Press, 1909.

Myriam, Harry, *Djelale Ddine Roumi, Poète et danseur mystique*, Paris, Flammarion, 1947.

Nicholson, R. A., *Studies in Islamic Mysticism*, Cambridge University Press, 1921.

Nicholson, R. A., *A Literary History of the Arabs*, New York, Charles Scribner & Sons, 1907.

Richter, G., *Persiens Mystiker Dschelal-Eddin Rumi; eine Stildeutung in drei Vortragen*, Breslau, 1953.

Rumi, Jalalalddin, *Divan-i Shams Tabriz, Selected Poems*, ed. and trans. R. A. Nicholson, Cambridge, 1898.

Rumi, Jalal-ud-Din, *Mathnawi*, trans. R. A. Nicholson, Vols II and IV, London, Luzac, 1926 and 1934 respectively.

Shabistari, M., *Gulshan I Raz* (*The Mystic Rose Garden*), trans. E. H. Whinfield, London, Trubner, 1880.